FPC

PRACTICE & REVISION KIT

FPC 3

Identifying and Satisfying Client Needs

- This **Practice & Revision Kit** contains advice and commentary on exam technique which is essential to ensure that you are prepared for the exam.

- A **technical review** highlights the required knowledge for this exam and allows candidates to identify weaknesses.

- **Three mock exams** ensure your final preparation is focused on the task in hand – success.

UPDATES ARE AVAILABLE ON OUR WEBSITE AT:

www.bpp.com

BPP Publishing
June 2000

Second edition June 2000

ISBN 0 7517 9814 2 (previous edition 07517 9809 6)

British Library Cataloguing-in-Publication Data
*A catalogue record for this book
is available from the British Library*

Published by

*BPP Publishing Limited
Aldine House, Aldine Place
London W12 8AW*

www.bpp.com

All our rights reserved. No part of this publication may be reproduced, stored in a retrieval system or transmitted, in any form or by any means, electronic, mechanical, photocopying, recording or otherwise, without the prior written permission of BPP Publishing Limited.

We are grateful to the Chartered Insurance Institute for permission to reproduce in this Kit references to the syllabus of which the Institute holds the copyright.

©
*BPP Publishing Limited
2000*

CONTENTS

	Page number
Introduction	(iv)
Using this Practice & Revision Kit	(iv)
Revision Guide	
How to revise	(v)
The exam	(vi)
Exam technique	(x)

Section A Answering questions

Chapter 1 Exam structure and technique requirements	3
Chapter 2 How to answer question 1	5
Chapter 3 How to answer question 2	13
Chapter 4 How to answer question 3	17

Section B Technical review

Chapter 5 Savings and investment products	31
Chapter 6 Protection review	37
Chapter 7 Pensions review	41

Section C Mock Exams

Mock Exam 1	49
Mock Exam 2	61
Mock Exam 3	73
Mock Exam 1 solutions	87
Mock Exam 2 solutions	99
Mock Exam 3 solutions	107

Order Form

Review Form & Free Prize Draw

Introduction

Welcome to BPP's 2000 FPC Practice & Revision Kits

You're taking professional exams. You're under time pressure to get your exam revision done, and trying to fit in study as well as a social life around your job is difficult. Could you make better use of your time? Are you sure that your revision is really relevant to the exam you will be facing?

If you use BPP revision material you can be sure that the time you spend revising and practising questions is time well spent. Our **Practice & Revision Kits** are clear, concise and effective and are focused exclusively on what you, the candidate, can expect to encounter in your exam.

- We offer **guidance on revision, question practice and exam technique** gleaned from years helping students to pass their FPC exams.

- We highlight the format of the exam that you will face and ensure that all of the **exam standard questions in the Kit** reflect that format.

- We ensure that **the mock exams are comprehensive** so that you can cover all areas of the syllabus if you have time.

- We provide **a technical review** which tests your knowledge and understanding of the syllabus and enables you to see whether or not you really are ready to begin practice and revision.

Using this Practice & Revision Kit

The kit is arranged in three sections.

Section A	Answering questions
Section B	Technical review
Section C	Mock exams

You should read through the **answering questions** section carefully since exam technique is as important as technical knowledge in ensuring exam success at FPC3.

The **technical review** gives you the opportunity to revise the critical knowledge areas examined at FPC3, namely pensions and taxation.

Your preparation can then be rounded off with the three mock exams which you should attempt under exam conditions.

The advice we provide, together with the **mock exams** offer you everything you need to ensure success. If you work diligently using this material you place yourself in the best possible position of achieving your goal – exam success.

REVISION GUIDE

How to revise

This is a very important time as you approach the exam. You must remember three things.

> **Use time sensibly**
> **Set realistic goals**
> **Believe in yourself**

Use time sensibly

1. **How much study time do you have?** Remember that you must EAT, SLEEP, and of course, RELAX.

2. **How will you split that available time between each subject?** What are your weaker subjects? They need more time.

3. **What is your learning style?** AM/PM? Little and often/long sessions? Evenings/weekends?

4. **Are you taking regular breaks?** Most people absorb more if they do not attempt to study for long uninterrupted periods of time. A five minute break every hour (to make coffee, watch the news headlines) can make all the difference.

5. **Do you have quality study time?** Unplug the phone. Let everybody know that you're studying and shouldn't be disturbed.

Set realistic goals

1. Have you set a **clearly defined objective** for each study period?
2. Is the objective **achievable**?
3. Will you **stick to your plan**? Will you make up for any **lost time**?
4. Are you **rewarding yourself** for your hard work?
5. Are you leading a **healthy lifestyle**?

Believe in yourself

Are you cultivating the right attitude of mind? There is absolutely no reason why you should not pass this exam if you adopt the correct approach

- **Be confident** - you've passed exams before, you can pass them again
- **Be calm** - plenty of adrenaline but no panicking
- **Be focused** - commit yourself to passing the exam

Revision guide

The exam

Paper 3 brings together Papers 1 and 2 with an emphasis on the identifying and satisfying client needs. It comprises **three case studies** each with a number of questions. No new technical knowledge is required, however your knowledge of taxation and pensions must be very keen. You need a good general understanding of the broad syllabus rather than detailed specific knowledge.

In the exam candidates will be expected to include specific consideration of:

- Taxation
- Risk
- Flexibility
- Affordability
- Need to monitor and review
- The reasons why a specific course of action has been recommended
- Suitability

Clients' needs have to be considered rather than looking for openings to **sell** specific products.

Structure of the exam

3 hours
3 questions, written test

Q1 Assessing client needs, fact finding (50 marks)

- Detailing all relevant data in the case study
- Listing questions to clarify inconsistencies and apparent errors

Q2 Providing advice (75 marks)

- Explanation of technical features relating to a fact find
- Recommending suitable products and course of action

Q3 Portfolio design (50 marks)

- Recommending and explaining a suitable portfolio or advising on an existing portfolio

All recommendations regarding products are to be drawn from a provided product list. (Sample product lists are provided in the mock exams in this kit.)

Pass mark: Sufficient to pass the expected standard of a practitioner offering advice with one year's unaccompanied but supervised experience, ie = 55%.

The paper is marked out of 175 total marks therefore you need about 97 marks.

Marking: Papers are marked using a positive marking system based on a specific marking scheme. No marks are deducted for incorrect answers. The marking guides provided to the mock exams are indicative of the style employed by the CII.

Revision guide

Analysis of past exam topics

The table below outlines the main topics and the scenarios examined.

	Question 1 (fact find)	Question 2 (technical)	Question 3 (portfolio)
JULY 1999	Couple, one self employed, one employed Pension details and financial objectives Knowledge of spouse's pension benefits, tax allowances, ISA limits was required	One employed, one self employed Pension planning Calculate benefits, additional contributions Protection planning to protect against long term disability Writing bonds in trust Benefits of paying off mortgage.	Retired couple Income around the level of the age allowance trap Wish to generate income of £3,000 per annum Cautious to moderate risk with some exposure to stock market No high or speculative investments
JULY 1998	Couple, self employed Business expansion Pension details Financial objectives	Self employed Pension planning Life assurance PHI/CII	Widow 68 £214,000 portfolio Income requirement Estate planning
JUNE 1997	Widowed mother Self employed Pension details Financial objectives	Couple Pension transfer PHI/CII	Widower 67 £60,000 portfolio Income requirement Capital protection
JULY 1996	Low paid on various benefits Pension details Life assurance	Employee OPS - FSAVC - AVC PHI	Review of a portfolio Creation of a portfolio/ Tax implications.
MARCH 1996	Self employed Pension details Tax objectives	Employee Mortgage application	HR taxpaying couple £120,000 to invest in higher risk assets Investment and unit trusts.
FEBRUARY 1996	Self employed, Mortgage, Pension details	Employee re OPS Self-employed re PPP Carry forward	44 yr. old, single, £100,000, ½ high risk, ½ low risk, tax efficiency
DECEMBER 1995	Employed, Mortgage, Pension, Endowment	Employee re OPS, AVCs, FSAVCs, Portfolio, Protection	75 yr. old, widowed, No risk investment, £50,000, tax efficient Future plans for income
SEPTEMBER 1995	Employed, Mortgage, Pension	Employee re OPS Transfer to PPP, IHT calculation	25 yr. old, about to marry, £100,000, needs £50,000 in 5 - 10 yrs, appreciates risk/return
JUNE 1995	Employee, OPS and FSAVC, Self employed, no pension, provide for grandkids' education	Couple employed, both teachers in Scheme. Considering changing endowment to repayment	55 yr. old, single, retiring, £20,000 annuity, £80,000 lump sum to invest for extra income of £200 pm. Tax efficiency
MARCH 1995	Couple, both in OPS, husband has other earnings. Considering for discounted rates	Couple needing protection	56 yr. old, male, single, £50,000 to invest for retirement. Protection products requirement.

(vii)   BPP Publishing

Revision guide

Summary of past exam topics

A clear pattern has emerged which provides candidates with advance warning of the technical skills required for exam success. You must have good knowledge of **pensions** and the **taxation** of investments and you must be able to **design a portfolio**. This Practice and Revision Kit has been designed to help you in this task.

Examiner's comments

An important insight can be obtained from the analysis of the examiner's comments regarding exactly what efforts will generate a pass mark – and what efforts will earn scant rewards.

- *March 1995*

    Candidates did not make best use of their time.

    - Not reading the whole question before answering
    - Repeating answers to subsequent parts of the question
    - Not answering the question set
    - Not applying knowledge in the most appropriate way.

- *June 1995*

    Candidates failed to do themselves justice.

    - Poor time planning
    - Not reading the question set
    - Providing superfluous information
    - Not recognising the significance of the mark allocation
    - Poor at seeking information.

- *September 1995*

    Some candidates prepared poorly.

    - Poor ability to structure 'fact find' answers
    - Sparse technical knowledge (on pension transfers)
    - Poor ability to 'explain' products
    - Not recognising the significance of the mark allocation.

- *December 1995*

    Technical knowledge was sound but candidates still had difficulty in explaining and evaluating points.

    Poor question reading led to a lot of easy marks being lost.

- *March 1996*

    Many candidates did not prepare for the exam.

    The key to success is applying broad knowledge to the case facts. More candidates managed their time effectively by taking note of the mark allocation.

- *July 1996*

    Poor exam technique coupled with limited tax knowledge led to weak performance. The presentation of answers left a lot to be desired and many answers were insufficiently detailed.

Revision guide

- *June 1997*

    Candidates failed to relate their answers to the information given in the question.

    - Poor knowledge regarding taxation of investments
    - Poor knowledge of pension transfer
    - Insufficient detail provided when making recommendations

- *July 1998*

    Candidates lost marks by not including sufficient information in their answers.

    - Poor knowledge regarding the tax treatment of investments

- *July 1999*

    Q1 Transferring the married couple's allowance would not make any difference to the overall tax position of the couple.

    The spouse pension was stated incorrectly and was spotted by most candidates.

    Candidates did not explain the ISA error.

    Candidates who did badly did so because the answers lacked depth. They did not ask enough questions or they just restated facts. The aim of this section should be to get further information from the client.

    Q2 A number of mistakes were made on the calculation of maximum pension because people used the wrong number of years. It was not known that AVC payments could include any overtime (or benefits in kind).

    Candidates failed to give specific recommendations when answering questions.

    Tax treatment of insurance funds and unit trusts was poor, as was the knowledge of use of writing a bond in trust.

    The implications of paying off a mortgage caused difficulties.

    Q3 Most candidates did well, spotting that the income was near the age allowance limit.

    Marks were lost when candidates did not show who owned the assets. The tax treatment of products was often omitted or it was given incorrectly.

    Growth products, eg National Savings Certificates, were often used in the portfolio, but the aim of the portfolio was to produce **income**.

    Answers often lacked depth on explanation. A narrow range of products was used in the portfolio.

Summary of the examiner's comments

Looking through these comments you should notice that the examiner puts as much emphasis on exam technique as technical knowledge. Indeed, it is evident that broad knowledge allied with good technique will result in exam success.

Revision guide

Exam technique

Passing professional examinations is half about having the knowledge, and half about doing yourself full justice in the examination. You must have the right technique.

The day of the exam

1. Set at least one **alarm** (or get an alarm call) for a morning exam.
2. Have **something to eat** but beware of eating too much; you may feel sleepy if your system is digesting a large meal.
3. Allow plenty of **time to get to the exam hall**; have your route worked out in advance and listen to news bulletins to check for potential travel problems.
4. **Don't forget** pens, pencils, rulers, erasers.
5. Put **new batteries** into your calculator and take a spare set (or a spare calculator).
6. **Avoid discussion** about the exam with other candidates outside the exam hall.

Technique in the exam hall

Time management

For those candidates who have not taken a written examination paper recently, time management is perhaps the most important skill to develop in order to ensure success at FPC 3.

The time available to complete the exam is 3 hours. There are 175 marks in total available in the exam therefore you need to allocate about **1 minute to acquire each mark**.

The better prepared you are, the quicker you will be able to get your ideas down on paper. Time can be gained on the first question as the answers required are not as involved as those required in both questions two and three.

Each sub-section of the exam is allocated a total of marks available and you should spend an appropriate amount of time in accordance with the marks that are available for that section. For example, if a sub-section of a question is given 12 marks you know that you will have approximately 12 minutes to answer this section. If you spend four minutes it is a good guide that you have not answered the question in the depth required by the examiner and, equally, if you have spent 25 minutes you will have answered in too much detail.

Ideally you should allocate some time at the end of the exam to read through your answers and correct any obvious mistakes that you have made.

You must be ruthless with your time. Once you have exceeded the time allocated to the question, you must leave some space (so you can come back later if you have a few spare moments) and move on to the next question. It is **easier to acquire marks at the start of a question rather than at the end of the question.**

The marking guide

Your paper will be marked by someone using a pre-prepared marking guide. Marks are awarded on a positive basis with no marks being deducted for incorrect comments. In order to meet the requirements of the marker we outline below key failings of candidates, failings which you should avoid!

Common failings of candidates in this paper

- Not reading the question properly and therefore wasting time writing about issues not requested in the question or a question that has not been set! Alternatively candidates repeat themselves because they do not take the precaution of reading all the requirements first.

- Often candidates do not give all of the *steps in a calculation*. You need to be aware that there are marks awarded for each step. This is critical. Even if you get the final answer wrong, you will get marks for the correct approach.

- If you are asked to make a recommendation this is all the examiner requires it is not required (unless specifically asked for) to go on and explain the pros and cons of each option. Provide justification for your recommendation, but do not ramble on about alternatives.

- When the candidate is asked to list, this is all the examiner wants. There is no need to provide any explanation of the items contained in the list.

- Where a candidate does not have the technical ability to answer the question they tend to 'waffle'. No marks are awarded to 'waffle' it would be better to spend the time elsewhere improving other answers. Saying that, you should always guess if you can't recall the answer. Remember, there is no negative marking.

- Poor presentation of answers leads to weak performance. Use headings, use bullet points, use a new link for each new statement.

In the exam

- You should consider how your time is best spent.

- Skimming through the questions before you get started is a good idea because it helps to settle your nerves, and it allows you to plan which questions you are going to attempt first. Reading all the requirements first will also prevent you from repeating yourself. The examiner will often ask questions which are asking fairly similar things and unless you read through all the requirements you may end up wasting valuable time.

- You should not leave the exam room if you finish within three hours. Try to improve the answers you have given. Read through the material and correct for obvious mistakes.

- There are no 'golden areas' in this exam. You only have to get an overall pass mark, and it is not possible to get a sectional fail. So don't worry if you cannot do a part of a question. Have a guess, then move on.

- Use bullet points to answer the questions set. A bullet point is a grammatically correct sentence which simply conveys the answer required. In many cases you don't even have to do this. If the examiner requires you to 'list' or 'outline', you can give single word answers. There is no need to repeat the question, the examiner knows what this is, so don't waste time copying it out or including it in the introduction to your answer.

- When asked to give advantages and disadvantages or compare and contrast items, it is a good idea to draw up a table and show the items placed at the side of each other. This will help the examiner mark your answer. It is often easier if you are using a table to present it in landscape format rather than the portrait approach invited by the answer book.

- As a general rule of thumb give one bullet point for each mark that is available.

Section A
Answering questions

Chapter 1

EXAM STRUCTURE AND TECHNIQUE REQUIREMENTS

1 EXAMINATION TECHNIQUE GENERALLY

1.1 The FP3 examination requires technique as much as knowledge. A failure to apply proper technique is likely to end in disaster. The nature of the questions is quite well defined. It is possible to pinpoint certain areas of technique which should help candidates avoid the most common pitfalls. We offer no apology here for reinforcing key exam techniques.

Style of answers

1.2 (a) You do not need to write essays. Use a bullet point style to highlight your points succinctly. Bullet points are grammatically correct sentences which make one point.

(b) Avoid being ambiguous.

Don't make statements such as 'Short term for asset backed investments.'

Put yourself in the shoes of the marker. What could this mean? A better alternative might be: The term is too short for asset backed investments.

This version is slightly longer, but unambiguous and would earn good marks.

Better still, be comprehensive. You could extend this by stating:

- Minimum 5 years time horizon required for asset backed investments
- Because of volatility of market value and income levels

Planning

1.3 Time is very tight in this exam.

(a) Because of this, there is a temptation to put one's head down and start writing without thinking or planning. DO NOT FALL INTO THIS TRAP. If you do, you will:

- Not answer the question set
- Produce confused and inefficient answers

(b) DO THIS

- Think
- Plan
- Analyse
- Arrange
- Conclude
- Present

Part A: Answering questions

(c) You will answer the question set and not the one you hoped, or thought had been set if you:

- Read all the requirements
- Read the client profile
- Read the requirements again

Use of time

1.4 The examination lasts for three hours and is marked out of 175 marks. As a broad guide therefore, this works out at roughly one mark per minute.

The exam paper will also give you a guide as to how much time it is expected you would spend on each question. You should treat this guide as approximate, but **avoid going over time at all costs**. This is vital, in particular when you are attempting question 1, which is relatively straightforward and can lead to some candidates writing too much.

Justification of recommendations

1.5 You are normally expected to justify recommendations.

(a) If you are not specifically asked to do so, it is still worthwhile making brief justifications.

(b) The reason for this is straightforward, in that the examiner will have a marking scheme which incorporates a certain amount of flexibility, but he will want to be sure that your recommendations are soundly based.

2 STYLE OF QUESTIONS

2.1 Questions follow a prescribed format.

Q1	Factfinding
Q2	Technical and recommendations
Q3	Portfolio planning.

2.2 The detail of each question in each exam will vary, but the descriptions and comments in Chapters 2, 3 and 4 should help you prepare for the style of questions you can reasonably expect.

Chapter 2

HOW TO ANSWER QUESTION 1

ANSWERING QUESTION 1

Question 1 always follows the same format. A case study is given, perhaps 400 words and you need to develop the skills and techniques necessary to meet the requirements which are these. You will have to:

(a) Repeat data from the question on personal, financial, pension or mortgage details and objectives

(b) Outline errors and inconsistencies (ie spot the error and give the reasoning why it is an errors)

(c) Ask questions necessary to establish a clear full picture of the position of the objectives in the question, eg retirement planning

1 REQUIREMENT 1

1.1 This requirement merely asks you to repeat data given in the case study. Most commonly, you need to cover pension and financial details. The trick here is to read the requirements first, then read the case study. This way you answer the question in a more efficient manner. (A highlighter is useful.)

1.2 Pension details will include:
- Nature of scheme
- Length of service
- Basis of contributions
- Life assurance benefits
- Provision for spouse/dependants

1.3 You must be specific and comprehensive. For example do not simply state that the pension is a final salary scheme. State the accrual rate, how many years service and the anticipated retirement age.

Objectives and priorities

1.4 In some cases the objectives will be precisely defined. For example, the client may wish to give £100,000 to his children on their 21st birthday.

In other cases, the objective may be defined, but with less precision; for example, sufficient money in retirement to allow the client to travel around the world.

You may also need to state the 'attitudes' of the clients.

(a) Attitude to risk
- No risk
- Balanced risk

(b) Attitudes in other areas
- Increase income
- Growth of tax
- Reduction of tax
- Ethical investments

Notes **Part A: Answering questions**

Note that marks will be available for all such points. You simply need to repeat what is given in the case study. The style of your answer should be very brief points, in most cases a simple statement of fact.

2 REQUIREMENT 2

Errors and inconsistencies

2.1 The second part of question 1 will require you to identify errors and inconsistencies. Your ability to identify errors and inconsistencies will depend on your technical knowledge and reading skills.

2.2 Errors and inconsistencies arise for the following reasons.
- Incorrect, ie there is an error
- Incomplete - information refused
- Conflicting views - husband and wife
- Opinions conflicting with current financial planning
- Misunderstanding

2.3 To gain full marks you should:
- Identify the error/inconsistency
- Explain why this is an error/inconsistency
- Where appropriate explain why this may have arisen
- Explain the correct treatment

2.4 Note that you do not need to distinguish between an error/inconsistency. If you think it is wrong, put it down. However, don't go fishing for 'subjective' inconsistencies. The examiner is primarily testing your technical knowledge.

3 REQUIREMENT 3

3.1 The third part of question 1 will involve asking questions which will elicit more information on the areas of concern in the scenario.

3.2 Two types of question you can ask are **closed** questions and **open** questions.

3.3 Closed questions are those which are designed to elicit a specific piece of information, such as a date of birth, or an income figure. Closed questions can gather accurate information in a short time, but not complete information. **The examiner wants you to ask the type of questions you would use in practice.**

3.4 **Open questions** give the client the opportunity to express his views, or his feelings, and invite a longer response.

(a) Examples might be:
- 'What are the schools like in this area?' or
- 'How do you feel about investments which can go down as well as up in value?'

(b) Questions of this sort give you information which can help you identify the considerations which are important to your client, and can give clues as to how he would react to different recommendations.

(c) Note you must **write the question** as though you are addressing the client.

3.5 You must also ask questions which are **understood by your client**.

(a) Abbreviations, as well as technical terms, are bound to confuse, so asking 'Are you a member of a PPS?' is not likely to be a productive question.

(b) **Avoid jargon,** and always aim to make sure that your questions are understandable, taking into account your client's level of knowledge and awareness of financial matters.

(c) The **order and progression** of questions is important too. For example, if you ask 'Have you got enough life cover?' or 'Are you happy with your investments?' the answer is likely to be 'Yes'. Otherwise, the client would presumably have done something about it.

3.6 Avoid questions which criticise the client.

3.7 Questions should be succinct and direct, but unambiguous.

3.8 The following are examples of questions to ask in various scenarios and are typical of the style employed in the examination guides. (It is a good idea to learn these questions by rote.)

Pensions

- How much income will you require in retirement?
- At what age would you like to retire?
- Do you have a pension currently or have you ever had any pension provision?
- Does your pension provide widows/dependant's pension?
- Are you entitled to full state pension?
- Are there any early retirement penalties if you take your pension at 60?
- What is the transfer value of your pension?
- May I see your pension scheme booklet?
- Do you pay any extra contributions?

Protection

- Other than the endowment policy, is there any life assurance on your life?
- How much would you need if you couldn't work due to ill health?
- May I see the protection/insurance scheme document?
- Do you know the levels of state benefits?
- Do you wish to rely on state benefits?
- Do you have any health problems?

Investments

- What investments/savings do you have?
- How much of your capital would you like access to?
- With regard to investing would you describe yourself as cautious or speculative?
- What are your income requirements from your capital?
- Do you want the investments in single or joint names?
- Are you concerned about the affects of inflation on your investments?

Savings for specific needs, eg education

- How much will school fees cost?
- When do you wish to start private education?
- How long do you wish to send x to school/university?
- How much can you afford to save each month?

Mortgage
- How much do you wish to borrow?
- Can you clarify what type of mortgage you have?
- Can I see your mortgage details?
- What is the value of your outstanding mortgage?
- When will the mortgage be repaid?
- Are you concerned about rises in interest rates?
- Are there any penalties if you repay the mortgage early?
- Have you asked the building society if you can reduce your payments/extend the term?

Capital/income tax
- How much income do you receive from your savings/investments?
- What income does your spouse have?
- Why are the investments in your name?
- Would you be willing to put investments in your spouse's name?
- Are you willing to tie up your capital for 5 years?

Inheritance tax
- Have you made a will?
- What is the value of your estate?
- Who would your beneficiaries be?
- Are all your assets jointly owned?
- Is the life policy/whole of life in trust?
- Have you made use of the nil rate band exemption?

2: How to answer question 1

Example of a typical question 1

The following is an example of a typical question 1. Attempt it under exam conditions and then study the recommended solution. Question 1 will always be in this format, so will the solution. If you have attempted it once you should have a good idea of the real thing.

Question 1 example

John Goodwin and his wife Mary came to see you last week. The following case history is based on your meeting with them. Read this carefully then carry out all of the tasks set out in (a), (b) and (c) below.

Information

John Goodwin aged 43, and his wife, Mary Goodwin, 40, have provided you with lots of information regarding their current personal and financial circumstances.

John is a self-employed web-site designer. He set up two years ago and works only part-time. He earned £27,000 last year and expects to earn a similar amount in the current tax year.

Mr Goodwin has a personal pension plan with a mutual insurance company into which he pays a net contribution of £150 each month by direct debit. He also made a single premium of £1,700 at the end of the tax year. He has written the policy to retire at age 65.

Mary Goodwin is employed by Network Computing Limited and is a programmer earning £40,000. She belongs to the company's occupational scheme which is a final salary scheme based on 1/80th of final salary for each year of service. The scheme is contributory and she pays in 7% of her salary. The benefits of the scheme include a spouse's pension of 80% of her salary and death in service benefits of two-and-a-half times final salary.

Both Mr and Mrs Goodwin have stated that they wish to plan for early retirement and retirement planning is therefore their major priority.

Mr Goodwin wishes to take a home study degree in Information Technology with the Open University. They wish to take a touring holiday of India next year for at least two months (Mrs Goodwin intends to take unpaid leave).

They also wish to move to a bigger property in the near future. There is substantial equity in their current property and they are worried that there will be a capital gains tax liability on the eventual sale. They have heard that is possible to fix the cost of a mortgage and are considering a three year capped rate as a way of achieving this.

Tax efficiency is also an important consideration and they have both made declarations to their respective building societies so that the interest from their savings accounts can be paid without the deduction of tax at source. They intend to pay any tax due at the end of the tax year.

An endowment policy has recently matured providing Mr and Mrs Goodwin with a lump sum of £50,000. They intend to use this sum to make use of tax efficient investments. They wish to contribute £7,000 each for each of the next three years at least into ISAs and they wish to create a tax-free income by investing in National Savings Income Bonds.

They have no other protection policies, other than the company benefits stated for Mrs Goodwin. They are particularly interested in income protection policies.

Questions Marks

(a) Under the following headings make notes on the information provided.

    (i) Pension details (6)
    (ii) Mr and Mrs Goodwin's financial objectives (7)

(b) **Identify** and **explain** and errors and inconsistencies in the information provided above. (12)

(c) Provide a list of questions that you would wish to ask Mr and Mrs Goodwin in order to ascertain all of the information that you would require to advise them further on:

    (i) Retirement planning (12)
    (ii) Their other financial objectives as identified in (a)(ii) above (13)

Part A: Answering questions

To attain the maximum marks possible you should write the questions in a way that can be understood by Mr and Mrs Goodwin.

Model Answer

(a) (i) *Pension details*

- Mr Goodwin has a personal pension plan into which he pays £150 every month.
- The pension is written to age 65.
- A single premium of £1,700 was paid into the plan at the end of the last tax year.
- Mrs Goodwin is a member of a final salary pension scheme (1/80th).
- She has to contribute 7% of her salary to the scheme.
- The scheme also provides the additional benefits of a spouse's pension and death in service benefits.

(ii) *Financial objectives*

- Mr and Mrs Goodwin want to retire early.
- They therefore wish to increase their current pension provision to achieve this objective.
- They wish to move to a bigger property in the near future.
- Mr Goodwin wishes to take an IT degree with the Open University.
- They wish to travel around India next year for two months.
- They wish to take out an income protection policy.
- They also want to make tax efficient investments in ISAs and National Savings Income Bonds.

(b) *Errors and inconsistencies*

Full marks could be obtained by identifying and explaining any six of the following.

Error	Inconsistency
Mr Goodwin states that he pays contributions into his PPP net.	Self-employed people pay contributions gross to a PPP.
Mrs Goodwin states that the spouse's pension under her scheme is 80% of her salary.	The maximum allowed under Inland Revenue regulations is 2/3rds of the maximum pension at normal retirement.
They think that there will be CGT on the sale of their current property.	The Principal Private Residence is exempt from capital gains tax.
They think that a capped mortgage will fix costs.	A cap places a maximum amount on the monthly payment for the period of the cap but does not fix costs. The cost of the mortgage can vary below the level at which the cap is set.
They have filled in gross interest declarations.	Only a non-taxpayer may have interest paid gross. Taxpayers must have interest paid with 20% tax deducted.
They wish to contribute £7,000 each to their ISAs for the next three years.	They may only contribute £7,000 this year (2000/01) and then £5,000 for each succeeding tax year.
They believe that the National Savings Income Bond provides tax free interest.	The Income Bond pays monthly income gross but it is not free of tax.

(c) (i) *Retirement planning.* Candidates would have gained full marks for giving any 12 of the following.

Mr Goodwin

- Could you tell me when you began your personal pension?
- May I see your personal pension contribution certificate in order to confirm the amount that you are paying into the scheme?
- Would it be possible for you to provide me with a profit forecast for the next three years?

Mrs Goodwin

- May I see your benefit statement from your scheme?
- May I see the scheme booklet and any information you have been given on the AVC scheme?
- Do you know if your scheme has been contracted out of SERPS?
- Do you intend to leave your current employers in the near future?

To either of Mr and Mrs Goodwin

- At what age would you like to retire?
- How much income do you think you will require in retirement?
- Do you have any pension that you have accumulated from previous periods of employment or self-employment?
- Do you know whether or not you will be entitled to a full state pension? (Have you always worked and paid national insurance would be a good indication that this is the case?)
- How much do you think you can set aside each month in order to boost your pension provision?
- Would it be better for you to make increased contributions on a monthly or annual basis?
- What other investments do you own that you could use to fund your retirement?
- Are there any other earnings from other sources, for example a second job or a furnished holiday let?
- How much risk would you be willing to take with your pension investments?

(ii) *Other financial objectives.* You would gain full marks for any 13 of the following list.

Moving house

- Will you require an additional mortgage when you move?
- Over what term will you require the additional mortgage, if any?
- What repayment method do you wish to use for the mortgage?
- When are you likely to want to move?

Open University degree for Mr Goodwin

- How many years will it take you to complete the degree?
- What will the fees be for this course?
- Do you wish to pay the fees as a lump sum or would you wish to pay in instalments from your income?
- Will the degree increase your earning prospects in the future?
- Will you be eligible for government grants to help with the funding of the degree?

Travelling to India

- When do you intend to take your sabbatical to India?
- How much is the holiday likely to cost?

Part A: Answering questions

Income protection
- What level of cover do you require?
- What are your fixed essential outgoings each month?
- Are you both in good health?
- Would you require a policy that provides replacement income or a lump sum?
- How long do you think you could get by from your own resources?
- What term would you wish the policy to cover you for?

Investments
- What level of risk would you be willing to take with your investments?
- Do you have a preferred term of investment?
- What level of emergency fund do you feel comfortable with?
- How much of the remaining funds would you wish to invest?

Chapter 3

HOW TO ANSWER QUESTION 2

1 TECHNICAL KNOWLEDGE

1.1 Question 2 tests your ability to **apply** technical knowledge and may also ask you to make recommendations from the product list included as part of the examination paper.

1.2 Question 2 will normally explore several different areas of financial planning, but will concentrate on one area normally pension planning, mortgages, or insurance.

1.3 Normally, there are many parts to Question 2, and you should ensure that you attempt each part.

2 TECHNIQUE

2.1 Use bullet points in your answer, and relate them to the question scenario, ie do not just scribble down everything you know about a certain key word.

For example, the question may ask about carry back of personal pension contributions.

- A **poor answer** would simply give the technicalities.
- A **good answer** would analyse the main points in the context of the cashflow and tax position of the individuals in the scenario.

2.2 **Explain your answer fully**. It is easy to fall into the trap of using expressions such as 'in the relevant tax year' or 'in the normal way'. The examiner will want you to demonstrate that you know which is the 'relevant' year, or what is the 'normal' way.

2.3 If the main focus of Question 2 is on an area in which you feel your knowledge is weak, then still attempt each part. The first few marks are always the easiest to achieve.

2.4 ALWAYS ATTEMPT EVERY PART OF THE QUESTION

2.5 Questions 2 and 3 will involve giving financial advice. You must consider the following factors.

- Affordability
- Priorities
- Attitude to risk
- Inflation
- Impact of taxation
- Potential for change
- Existing arrangements

Part A: Answering questions

3 AFFORDABILITY

3.1 However much a client may need a particular financial solution, unless he can afford the cost it entails, it cannot form part of a realistic recommendation.

3.2 Arrangements beyond a client's spending power are unlikely to achieve the client's objectives, and early termination is likely to lead to loss.

3.3 It is important to establish affordability in the:
   (a) Present context
   (b) Future to cope with changing circumstances

4 PRIORITIES

4.1 As it is unlikely that a client would be able to finance arrangements to meet all of his financial needs, the question of prioritisation is central to recommendations.

4.2 **Possible priority list for employed young married man**
   - Death insurance
   - Income protection
   - Pensions planning
   - Savings and investments

4.3 **Possible priority list for self employed single man**
   - Income protection
   - Pensions planning
   - Savings and investments

5 ATTITUDE TO RISK

5.1 Risk relates to security of capital **and** variability of income.

5.2 Your recommendations should include:
   - A description of the degree of risk involved in each investment under consideration
   - Details of what this actually means

6 INFLATION

6.1 The following aspects must be considered.
   - Ongoing review
   - Long term - match earnings inflation
   - Specific cost inflation eg school fees

7 IMPACT OF TAXATION

7.1 The usefulness of different investments will vary from client to client depending on their tax situation.

7.2 You should always remember that the attractiveness of a portfolio from the client's point of view will be largely judged according to the return he achieves after taxation, not before.

8 POTENTIAL FOR CHANGE

8.1 The portfolio and recommendations you make must allow some flexibility for changes in circumstances. The following factors will generate potential changes.

- Death
- Illness
- Divorce
- Children

8.2 Consequently you should consider the flexibility of products which giving advice. Products which reduce flexibility include:

- Fixed term insurance related investment contracts
- National savings certificates
- Annuities
- Guaranteed products
- Pensions

9 EXISTING ARRANGEMENTS

9.1 A client's existing arrangements will inevitably affect recommendations because they will impact upon the extent to which his needs in various areas are **already met**.

9.2 It is also important to take into account whether or not those existing arrangements **remain relevant** to the client's needs.

9.3 In most circumstances, it is inappropriate to terminate existing arrangements, particularly where this would entail a loss from the client's point of view. You must simply identify the weaknesses and the benefits (there will be some) of the current arrangements.

9.4 With existing investments, such as shares and unit trusts, there are also costs involved in sale and replacement.

9.5 In addition the effect of taxation on restructuring should be considered, particularly if it could lead to a liability to income tax or capital gains tax which would not otherwise have arisen, or would have been deferred.

Occupational pension and other benefits

9.6 In framing recommendations, you should also be aware of benefits associated with the individual's employment. Very often this will include pension and life assurance arrangements but there may also be other benefits including permanent health insurance and private medical insurance.

9.7 To the extent that these are funded by the employer, they will certainly be an extremely attractive benefit from the point of view of the employee. It would therefore be very unusual for it to constitute good advice to opt out of an employer based scheme in favour of private provision which the employee would normally have to fund entirely himself.

9.8 In preparing your recommendations, you would therefore seek to build on top of the benefits provided by the employer.

9.9 Employers do change the basis of benefits provided for employees from time to time, so as part of your ongoing review of your client's affairs, you would necessarily need to keep up to date with any such changes. In addition, the provision of benefits will almost certainly be dependent upon the continuation of employment and this therefore should also be kept under review.

Chapter 4

HOW TO ANSWER QUESTION 3

1 PORTFOLIO PLANNING

1.1 This question is intended to check your skill in constructing a portfolio to meet the specific requirements of a particular client.

1.2 You may be given details of an existing portfolio, or you may be asked to consider the investment of entirely new money, possibly arising from something like an inheritance or a pools win.

1.3 Details given may relate to:
- Requirements
- Risk attitude
- Income need

1.4 It is important to specify how **all** of the available money will be invested.

1.5 It will also include specifying **where money will be held** even if it is known that it will only be available temporarily for investment, for example, money for an imminent house move.

2 PRODUCT LIST AND TAX TABLES

2.1 The examination paper includes a product list and tax tables. Use them.

2.2 The tax tables may be useful to you in answering some or all of the questions. As well as details of income tax, inheritance tax and capital gains tax, the tables include some explanation of the workings of the taxes, for example, indexation for CGT purposes.

2.3 Allowable contributions for retirement annuities and personal pensions are also given.

2.4 Look through the content of the tables before you start the exam, so that you know what is available to you.

We include one at the back of the question bank and exams. The names are fictitious, but the tables follow the same format as in your exams.

2.5 The tables give investment limits where appropriate. Don't go over these limits, eg £10,000 in NSC. You will lose marks if these limits are exceeded, or if you use an incorrect rate of return in your answers, so again check what information you are given.

2.6 Although the product listing does not cover all possible products and investments, **only those included on the list should be used in your answers**. You will not be awarded marks for product recommendations not taken from the list, however suitable they might be.

Part A: Answering questions

3 DESIGNING AN INVESTMENT PORTFOLIO

3.1 You need to spend the money, but also explain your recommendations. Your technique should be as follows.

Step 1. Establish objectives
Step 2. Identify products which meet the objectives
Step 3. Justify your recommendations

3.2 The approach to take is best covered with question practice but we can outline some basic priorities.

Most (nearly all portfolios) will have the following components.

- Emergency fund
- TESSAs (if existing) (TESSA only ISA on maturity)
- NS Products
- Equity backed products using ISAs (dependent upon risk profile)

This is not an opportunity to sell products so do not just include commission earning products. If your portfolio has not got any NS products there has to be a good reason.

3.3 Take careful note of the **risk profile**. Your portfolio must relate to the client's attitudes to risk.

The following proportions are a guide only but reflect the equity weightings shown in examination guides.

	Equity exposure
Nil risk profile	0%
Low risk profile	20%
Balanced risk profile	30 - 40%
Willing to accept risk	<60%

Unless told otherwise, **never put the whole of the portfolio into equity/asset backed investments.**

4 ACCESSIBILITY

4.1 One of the primary considerations is the extent to which an investor is likely to require **access to the money** he has invested. The more money that is available, the more freedom there will be to invest in assets which are not immediately accessible but which are geared to provide the best possible return in the longer term.

4.2 A first priority in virtually all cases will be the establishment of an adequate **emergency fund** available immediately.

4.3 In theory you should use a figure of between three and six months' income.

In the exam you may use the following shortcut

£2,000 < £x < £20,000

£x is dependant upon:

- Risk
- Age
- Sum for investment

4.4 Even after establishing the emergency fund, further consideration needs to be given to accessibility to all investments. If the investment is not accessible say so.

5 INCOME AND CAPITAL GROWTH

5.1 The need to draw regular amounts by way of income from the investment will also be an important factor in determining the portfolio overall.

The balance will be determined by:
- Tax considerations
- Growth considerations
- Attitude to risk

Techniques to generate income

5.2 (a) Use guaranteed products - preferably National Savings products, for the majority of the income.

(b) Avoid variable income products, annuities and roll up products.

(c) Obtain diversification.

(d) Obtain the balancing amount from a bank or building society account.

(e) NB. You do not need the exact amount – but you should arrive at a figure that is close to the required amount.

Example

Mrs Smith 62 needs £5,000 more net income each year.

She is a basic rate taxpayer with other income of £8,000.

She has £120,000 to invest.

	Interest (Gross)	After Tax (20%)
NS Pensioners bond £50,000 @ 7%	3,500	2,800
NS Income bonds £28,000 @ 6.25%	1,750	1,400
Building Society £20,000 @ 5%	1,000	800
		5,000

You could use a private sector income bond. (Guaranteed income bond – but not for a non-tax payer as they are not able to reclaim tax paid.)

Notes

1 Not all of the £120,000 is used. She will have other objectives - but we have achieved her income requirement.

2 The savings income falls in the 22% band and is taxed at 20%.

Note that you should avoid generating income from tax efficient investments. The marking guides of the CII tend to imply that such income should be retained within the tax efficient wrapper.

Part A: Answering questions

6 RISK PROFILE

6.1

	Negligible risk	Low risk	Cautious	Medium risk	High risk	Speculative
Deposit based and similar investments	National Savings	Bank deposit Building Society Deposit TESSA Annuities				
Gilts *	Gilts (income) Gilts (redemption)		Gilts (pre-redemption capital value)			
Life insurance linked		Non-profit Guaranteed Income/ growth bonds	With profit	Unit-linked (managed) Unit-linked (UK funds)	Unit-linked (overseas funds)	
Equity investment				Unit trusts (UK) Investment trusts (UK)	Single UK equities Unit trusts (overseas funds) Investment trusts (overseas)	
Derivatives*						Futures Options

* Note there are no gilts or derivatives on the product list and therefore they will not feature in a specific portfolio. You may however get generic questions on such products in question 2.

Diversification

6.2 The portfolio will need to be diversified. This diversification will be across asset type *and* provider.

Consequently if you are placing significant funds in life assurance products, or unit trusts (significant being between £5,000 to £10,000) consider using more than one provider.

If substantial sums will be invested in equity based products (in excess of £20,000) consider international diversification.

You will get marks for recognising the need to diversify.

7 TAXATION

7.1 Investments producing a tax free return will be more attractive to higher rate taxpayers than to basic rate or indeed to non-taxpayers, and the higher rate taxpayer will therefore be more inclined to accept any accompanying limitations on accessibility or flexibility in return for those tax advantages.

7.2 Tax delayed is tax saved, and where the taxation position is likely to change in the foreseeable future, an arrangement such as an investment bond, which has the effect of deferring taxation liability might be extremely attractive.

8 COSTS

8.1 Different investments incorporate different levels of cost and inevitably this will be a factor which influences overall portfolio design.

8.2 Particularly if investment is intended only for the short term, any significant initial costs would seriously erode or even eliminate any potential return. On the other hand longer term investments should have time to recoup initial charges and the level taken into account in any recommendations.

9 REVISING AN INVESTMENT PORTFOLIO

9.1 Costs are also an important factor in deciding whether or not a portfolio should be reorganised.

Switching costs often outweigh the increase in yield or growth from new alternative investments.

The effect of capital gains tax

9.2 Whenever a portfolio is revised, care must be taken to ensure that any tax liability is fully taken into account. This does not just mean the taxation of the investments themselves, and any income they produce, but also includes the effect of CGT at the time of the revision.

9.3 If assets such as shares or unit trusts are sold, then a CGT liability can occur as a result. Any potential gain from investment performance may well be completely negated by any CGT liability that arises, and which could have been deferred or even avoided had the sale of some of the assets been at least delayed.

9.4 So, for example, a move from direct shareholdings to unit trusts, in order to improve the spread of investments and to benefit from professional management, could be achieved in stages to make use of the annual CGT exemption over a number of years.

Income tax

9.5 Similarly, on encashment of a single premium investment bond, a liability to higher rate tax could arise, which again needs careful handling. If the bond is segmented (ie consists of a number of constituent policies) it may be best to stagger encashment over a number of years, to avoid large gains falling in one year and creating a substantial higher rate tax liability.

9.6 If there is only one bond, it will be necessary to consider the effect of full or partial encashment, since the calculation of any gain for tax purposes is different in each case.

10 JUSTIFICATION

10.1 You must justify your recommendations. You can do this on the face of your portfolio or beneath depending upon the question requirements.

You may wish to use the following mnemonic to facilitate your justification.

10.2 Consider:

Flexibility
Earnings (ie income)
Access
Risk
Charges
Amount
Tax

4: How to answer question 3 Notes

Example of a typical question 3

We now provide you with a typical example of Question 3. Attempt it under exam conditions and then assess the model answer. Question 3 will always involve a portfolio planning element, so make sure you understand the method behind the model answer.

You should assume that the information provided in this question is accurate.

Case history: Simon and Sandy Rudkin   Married: aged 68 and 63 respectively

Need: Income but with potential for capital growth over the long term

Information

Mr and Mrs Rudkin both retired five years ago. They decided to retire at the same time so that they could enjoy travelling around the world together whilst they were still young enough to do so. They both love travelling and wish to be able to afford three or four trips abroad each year.

They have two grown up sons and no other financial dependants.

Financially they are 'comfortable'. Mr Rudkin receives an occupational pension from the Civil Service (which is index linked) as well as the State Pension. His total income is £17,500 gross. Mrs Rudkin was a lecturer of History at Cleverland University and has a total annual pension income from the University and the state of £10,000.

They had a huge house close to the University that they recently decided to sell so that they could afford to buy a place in the Cotswolds. They used the proceeds of the sale to pay off their outstanding debt and to top up their deposit account with the internet bank 'Bacon'.

Now they have £200,000 in their joint account with Bacon. They have always been concerned about tax efficiency and have both fully utilised the TESSA allowance of £9,000. They both also have stocks and shares ISAs with £7,000 invested (in respect of the tax year 1999/2000). The TESSA accounts are due to mature in the coming month. The amount on maturity is expected to be £11,500 (which includes accrued interest of £2,500).

Mr Rudkin wishes to create an extra income of £8,000 net from their investments. They do wish that you also have consideration for capital growth in the long run. He is concerned that should he die his occupational pension will only provide an income of 50% his current pension to Mrs Rudkin. He would like the capital to be available to create an income for Mrs Rudkin in this eventuality.

They are both cautious to moderate risk investors. They are prepared to invest in blue chip stocks but do not wish to have any undue exposure to high risk or speculative stocks as they feel that they cannot afford to take this risk at their 'time of life'. They wish to continue with the theme of tax efficient investment and would like to provide their two sons with as much of their capital as possible after they have died.

Questions

(a) Provide a list of things that you would consider when drawing up your recommendations for Mr and Mrs Rudkin (11)

(b) Recommend, from the product list provided, a portfolio which meets Mr and Mrs Rudkin's needs. You should note that marks are awarded for showing the amount to be invested in each of your recommendations and who owns each of the investments. Show how you arrive at the income required (19)

(c) For each of the products used in your recommendation:
- Justify the amount that you have invested
- Comment on the risks involved with each of the investments
- State the reasons for your recommendation (15)

(d) Briefly, state how you would review this portfolio after it has been running for a year (5)

Total Marks (50)

Notes **Part A: Answering questions**

Suggested solution

(a) *Any 11 of the following would have obtained full marks*
- Simon Rudkin is 68 and Sandy Rudkin is 65.
- They both took retirement five years ago.
- Their financial need is to create an additional £8,000 of net income per annum.
- They also have a need for capital growth.
- Mr Rudkin's Civil Service pension will halve if he dies first leaving Mrs Rudkin with a very much reduced income.
- At present Mr Rudkin benefits from a slightly reduced age allowance (if we ignore the proceeds of the house sale which will create interest income).
- Mr Rudkin's age allowance is reduced by £250 as his income is £500 over the limit (it is reduced by £1 for every £2 that the limit is exceeded).
- They both have to pay income tax at the basic rate on their income (22% in the current tax year).
- They are happy to invest in cautious to moderate risk investments but wish to avoid high risk and speculative investments.
- The have a total of £223,000 to invest, £200,000 capital and £23,000 from the TESSAs
- Tax efficiency is important in the construction of the portfolio.
- Inheritance tax should be considered in the design of the portfolio as they wish to minimise the amount of tax paid on the second death.

(b) *The portfolio provided here is a suggestion. It is not necessarily a definitive answer. Provided you meet the client's requirements and show the examiner that you have good reasons for each product you will gain the marks that are available.*

Investment	Amount	Ownership	Risk	Term	Gross Yield	Net Yield	Income
Tinytown bank cheque account	£8,000	Joint	Low	N/a	1.8%	1.44%	£115
Townshires B/Soc 90 day	18,000	Mrs Rudkin	Low	N/a	6.2%	4.96%	£893
Existing TESSA	£11,500	Mr Rudkin	Low	Five Years*	7%	7%	N/a
Existing TESSA	£11,500	Mrs Rudkin	Low	Five Years*	7%	7%	N/a
Maxi ISA Solid UK	£7,000	Mr Rudkin	Moderate	Five Years +	4.1%	4.1%	£287
Maxi ISA High Income	£7,000	Mrs Rudkin	Moderate	Five Years +	5.2%	5.2%	£364
National Savings Certificates 51st Fixed	£10,000	Mr Rudkin	Low	Five Years	3.5%	3.5%	N/a
National Savings 15th Index-linked	£10,000	Mr Rudkin	Low	Five Years	RPI + 1.65%	RPI + 1.65%	N/a
National Savings Certificates 51st Fixed	£10,000	Mrs Rudkin	Low	Five Years	3.5%	3.5%	N/a
National Savings 15th Index-linked	£10,000	Mrs Rudkin	Low	Five Years	RPI + 1.65%	RPI + 1.65%	N/a
Central With Profits Bond	£20,000	Mrs Rudkin	Cautious	Five Years +	6% est.	6% est.	£1,200
Central Insurance GIB Five Year Fixed Rate	£25,000	Mrs Rudkin	Low	Five Years	6.4%	6.4%	£1,600
Fairplay insurance managed	£25,000	Joint	Moderate	Five Years +	6.8%	6.8%	£1,700
XYZ Gilt Fund	£25,000	Mrs Rudkin	Cautious	Five Years +	6.2%	4.96%	£1,240
XYZ Equity Income	£25,000	Mrs Rudkin	Moderate	Five Years +	4.2%	3.78%	£945

Total £223,000   £8,344

* Due to mature in the coming month

Part A: Answering questions

(c) *Deposit investments at the bank and building society*
- Funds can be held here for easy access.
- Funds held in the cheque account will provide instant access.
- The 90 day deposit account allows funds to be accessed within a reasonable period and the money is earning a good rate of return.

TESSA
- The maximum capital investment of £9,000 has already been made.
- There is no tax on interest if held for the full five year term.
- Due to mature within the month, when it would then be appropriate to reinvest the capital in a TESSA-Only ISA or the cash component of a maxi or a mini (this will not affect the overall annual contribution limits).

National Savings Certificates. Fixed and Index Linked Issues
- The investment is the maximum allowed for non-reinvestments.
- They are provided by an agency of the UK Government and therefore there is no default risk.
- There is a guaranteed real return on the index-linked certificates.
- The fixed interest certificate provides a tax free return (it does not have be shown on the tax return to the Inland Revenue).
- Access to capital is possible within the five year term, however, the best interest will be achieved if the investment is allowed to run for the full five years.

ISAs
- All proceeds in an ISA are free of income and capital gains tax.
- Mr and Mrs Rudkin are investing in maxi stocks and shares ISAs. These have the ability to reclaim the tax credits on dividends until April 2004.
- The value of investments can fluctuate.
- The investments selected will provide a fairly high level of tax free income but should also add capital growth in the long term.
- The maximum amount allowed by legislation has been suggested for each of the couple.

Investment bonds
- A with-profit bond is a cautious to moderate risk investment.
- It smoothes out the underlying volatility of the stock market.
- It can be used to take an income of up to 5% per annum without incurring an additional tax liability.
- The underlying investments are mainly comprised of equity so this should provide long term growth.
- The managed fund investment is designed to provide a return which is based on investment in equities, property and fixed interest funds according to the manager's view of future market conditions.
- This investment is moderate risk but can be used to take an income of 5% with no immediate tax consequences.
- As both Mr and Mrs Rudkin are basic rate tax payers, they may exceed the 5% allowance with no further tax due.
- The investments have been put in Mrs Rudkin's name so that the extra income generated does not affect Mr Rudkin's age allowance.
- The bonds should be written under a flexible trust so that Mr Rudkin and the two sons are possible beneficiaries, this could save IHT in the future.

4: How to answer question 3

Guaranteed income bond

- Capital is completely safe and is guaranteed to be returned at the end of this five year investment.
- Income is also guaranteed at the rate set at the beginning of the investment.
- The rate quoted is net of basic rate tax so there will be no further tax liability for Mr and Mrs Rudkin.
- Whatever happens to interest rates or the stock market Mr and Mrs Rudkin can be sure of this income.

Unit trusts

- Unit trusts will bring diversification to the portfolio.
- They are moderate risk and fit therefore fit the specifications of the client.
- They both provide the potential for income or long term capital growth.
- It is possible to offset any capital gains against the annual exemption for CGT.
- The gilt fund should provide a steady income and will be slightly less risky than an equity fund.

(d) At the next annual review the following should be considered.

- Has the annual subscription to ISA been utilised for both Mr and Mrs Rudkin?
- Is there a new issue of National Savings Certificates that you wish to utilise?
- Have the maturing TESSAs been reinvested?
- How are the investments performing?
- Is the required level of income being produced?
- Are there any changes in circumstances that need to be taken into account?
- Has tax or other legislation changed to affect the efficiency of the current investments?

Section B
Technical review

Chapter 5

SAVINGS AND INVESTMENT PRODUCTS

1 ASPECTS OF CHOICE

1.1 **Important aspects in the choice of products**
- Objectives
- Accessibility
- Tax treatment
- Risk profile

1.2 People's objectives will often be contradictory or incompatible so you need to:
- Identify objectives: income, capital growth, safety, simplicity etc.
- Satisfy, not maximise, these objectives
- Have graduated risk exposure

2 PRODUCT FEATURES

The following points are relevant in your justifications. LEARN THEM BY HEART.

2.1 Bank or building Society
- Emergency fund access
- Feeder TESSA (TESSAs may continue to be fed).
- Minimal risk (£20,000 investor protection fund)
- Postal notice account for better return
- Non taxpayers receive gross

2.2 NS Certificates Index Linked/Fixed Rate
- Inflation proofed
- Secure
- Tax free growth
- Roll up of interest
- Access with penalties

2.3 NS Pensioner's Bond
- Good rate of return
- Secure
- Accessible with penalties/on notice
- Guaranteed rate of interest
- Gross (taxable)
- Two and five year term

Part B: Technical review

2.4 NS Income Bond
- Good rate of return
- Secure
- Accessible with penalties
- Monthly income
- Gross

2.5 NS Capital Bond
- Good/higher rate of return
- Secure
- Accessible with penalties
- Rarely suitable for a higher rate taxpayer

2.6 Investment trusts/unit trusts
- Potential for long term/capital growth
- Spread of investment/risk/satisfies risk profile
- Gives exposure to equity markets
- Can give income to supplement pension
- Use of CGT allowance (£7,200 annual exemption)

2.7 GIB
- Secure income
- No further tax if basic rate tax payer
- Capital secure

2.8 TESSA (Existing TESSAs continue, no *new* TESSAs from 6th April 1999).
- Tax free interest
- Net interest can be taken
- Accessible if needed
- 5 year plan (last plan will mature in 2004)
- Secure
- Rollover into ISA or open up and keep for 5 years

2.9 Managed bond/with profits
- Potential for long term/capital growth
- Spread of investment/risk
- Switchability
- Secure/lower risk
- 5% tax deferred income facility
- No further tax if basic rate taxpayer

2.10 Offshore
- No withholding tax
- Gross income
- Growth
- Confidentiality
- Access to riskier investments

2.11 Gilts/corporate bonds
- Income taxed
- Capital growth tax free
- Secure if held to redemption

2.12 Individual Savings Accounts
- Tax free income
- Range of options: shares, cash or life assurance
- Ten year life (before legislation review)
- Tax free capital gains
- Annual limits
- Accessible
- CAT standards
- Choice of maxi or mini
- Matured TESSA can be invested in a TESSA-only ISA

3 INVESTMENT OBJECTIVES

3.1 Try to fill in the recommended products column to satisfy the following objectives.

OBJECTIVE	RECOMMENDED PRODUCTS
SHORT TERM CAPITAL GROWTH	
Quick capital gain	
Capital investment grows in value over 0 – 5 years	
LONG TERM CAPITAL GROWTH	
Capital to grow in value in 5 - 10 years or more	
INCOME NOW	
Immediate need for income	
INCOME LATER	
Income stream at later stage in life eg retirement	

Suggested solutions are given at the end of this chapter.

Notes   Part B: Technical review

4   INVESTMENT CONCERNS

4.1   Given the following concerns what products/advice would you recommend?

CONCERN	RECOMMENDED ADVICE
Inflation	
Unpredictability of returns	
Liquidity	
Timing of entry/exit	
High charges	
Need for simplicity	
Higher rate taxpayer	

Suggested solutions are given at the end of this chapter.

SOLUTIONS

3.1

OBJECTIVE	PRODUCTS
SHORT TERM CAPITAL GROWTH	
Quick capital gain	Single equities
Capital investment grows in value over 0-5 years	Guaranteed growth bond
LONG TERM CAPITAL GROWTH	
Capital to grow in value in 5-10 years or more	Invest in equity backed products UT/IT if risk is acceptable With profits if lower risk requirement
INCOME NOW	
Immediate need for income	Annuities Bank accounts Guaranteed income bonds (NS or insurance)
INCOME LATER	
Income stream at later stage, eg retirement	Pensions Deferred annuities Any capital growth product (preferably tax efficient) which can buy income in the future

4.1

CONCERN	RECOMMENDED ADVICE
Inflation	Index linking Equity backed investments generating real returns
Unpredicability of returns	Guaranteed products (NS)
Liquidity	Cash Unit trusts Single company investments (blue chip)
Timing	Regular premium
Charges	Avoid life insurance investment products
Simplicity	Cash, NS
Higher rate tax	Pensions, ISAs, TESSA-only ISA for matured TESSA proceeds, NSCs.

Chapter 6

PROTECTION REVIEW

1 PROTECTION PRODUCTS SUMMARY

1.1 The table below summarises the basic features of protection products. You should be familiar with all the contents.

Type	Objective	Trigger	Taxation
TERM	Loan payment/replace income on death	Death	None if qualifying
FAMILY INCOME	Replace salary on death	Death	Tax free income
WOL	Capital sum on death	Death	None if qualifying
UNIVERSAL	Complete cover	Death, accident, redundancy	Non qualifying from inception
CRITICAL ILLNESS	Peace of mind/buy income annuity	Diagnosis	Lump sum tax free
TERMINAL ILLNESS	Last chance of holiday/assistance in dying days	Diagnosis	Lump sum tax free, not written in trust
INCOME PROTECTION (PHI)	Replace salary 50%-66% cover	Stop work and disability	Tax free income. Cannot be used as NRE for pensions
PMI (Private Medical)	Medical costs cover	Hospital bills	Tax free benefit
LONG TERM CARE	Medical costs	Bills-in or out patient	• No relief • tax-free proceeds
REDUNDANCY	No salary to cover mortgage interest payments	Lose job	As PHI
ACCIDENT AND SICKNESS	Income if accident. Lump sum if lose limb	Accident	Lump sum tax free/taxed as PHI -2 years benefit max
WAIVER OF PREMIUM	Premiums/contributions paid if income is lost	Stop work	None

2 MAKING CHOICES: PROTECTION

2.1 For **life assurance**, much depends on the need being covered, and whether it is temporary or permanent. Likely changes in the level of cover required will determine whether an increasing or decreasing arrangement would be preferred.

2.2 Cost is often a primary concern. Given that most people cannot afford to provide as much cover as they would ideally have, the lower premiums associated with a term product can be attractive, and convertible term gives the option to move to 'whole life' later.

Part B: Technical review

2.3 For **health insurance**, income protection (PHI) should be seen as central, where this cover is not already provided by the employer. The self-employed particularly should see this as a priority. However, cost considerations could point towards the limited cover provided by sickness and accident insurance policies.

2.4 **Private medical insurance** is important for many people, but perhaps less so than PHI, since NHS treatment is available as an alternative.

2.5 **Long-term care** is also growing in popularity as the likelihood of a long life beyond retirement increases.

3 TAX TREATMENT OF LIFE POLICIES

3.1 **For the individual**

(a) The following must apply if the policyholder is to suffer income tax.

- Non-qualifying policy
- Chargeable event
- Chargeable gain
- Higher rate taxpayer

If someone 'buys' a policy, then on realising its value there could be a charge to capital gains tax.

(b) Examples of chargeable events

- Death of the life assured
- Total surrender of the policy
- Maturity of the policy
- Assignment of the policy for money or money's worth

Qualifying policies

3.2 For a term assurance to be qualifying, the following rules must apply.

(a) **Where the term is for 10 years or less**

- The term must be for at least one year.
- The policy must secure only a capital sum on death - no other benefits.

(b) **Where the policy is for over 10 years**

- The policy must secure only a capital sum on death - no other benefits.
- The premiums must be paid annually, or more frequently, for at least 10 years or 75% of the term whichever is shorter.
- The total premiums paid in any one year must not exceed twice the total premiums payable in any other year and one eighth of the total premiums payable over the whole term.

If these rules are followed, with the exception of a mortgage protection policy which is exempt, then the policy is treated as 'qualifying' for tax purposes.

Non qualifying policies

3.3 The principal example is a single premium bond.

For example, Michelle buys a single premium life policy for £20,000 at time 0. Cashes in the policy in year 7 for £34,000.

What is her tax position if her **taxable** income is:

(a) £26,900?
(b) £30,000?

Solutions are given at the end of the chapter.

SOLUTIONS

3.3 (a) Part of the gain will fall in the higher rate band so we must average the gain then top slice.

	£	£
Proceeds	34,000	
Premium	(20,000)	
Gain	14,000	
Average gain	$\frac{£14,000}{7}$	= 2,000

	£
Taxable income	26,900
Average gain	2,000
	28,900
Basic and lower rate bands	(28,400)
Amount of gain falling in higher rate band	500

Tax to pay = 500 × 18% × 7 = £630

(b) All the gain falls into the higher rate band, so no averaging is required.

14,000 × 18% = £2,520

Chapter 7

PENSIONS REVIEW

1 FACTORS DETERMINING PENSION REQUIREMENTS

Previous and current pension arrangements

1.1 Checking on the client's existing pension arrangements and his entitlement to the State pension is the first stage in the assessment process.

Basic state pension

1.2 The basic state pension is dependent upon sufficient NI Contributions being paid (for 90% of working life) and is currently £3,510 (00/01) for a single person.

State Earnings Related Pension Scheme

1.3 (a) The benefits of the State Earnings Related Pension are based on earnings **between** two bands. For 2000/01 these earnings bands are:

   (i) Lower earnings limit £3,484
   (ii) Upper earnings limit £27,820

   These earnings are the middle band earnings.

   (b) Earnings above the upper earnings limit will not be pensioned.

   (c) For those retiring between 1998 and 2000, the DSS will revalue each of their band earnings in line with inflation, take the best 20 years and then allocate a pension based on $1.25\% \times 20 = 25\%$ of the inflation proofed middle band earnings.

   (d) Those who have less than 20 years in the scheme, say 15, will simply have a calculation of $1.25\% \times 15$ of the inflation proofed middle band earnings.

   (e) From the year 2010, the maximum calculation will be reduced to 20% of middle band earnings of the average revalued middle band earnings throughout the member's whole working life.

Age

1.4 (a) The age at which the client wishes to retire is important The adviser needs to ascertain if is it 65, 60 or earlier.

   (b) If the client is older than the spouse, there may be a greater need to provide for an adequate pension for a widow or widower.

   (c) The current age of the client is also important. A young client has many years to achieve his or her objectives. The older the client, the fewer the years available and the more expensive the exercise becomes.

Notes   Part B: Technical review

2   PENSIONS SUMMARY

Type	NRA	Max Contribution	Max lump sum (Tax free)	Max annuity (taxable)	Death	Comments
1. STATE						
(i) Basic	60-65	National Insurance	None	£3,471 (£66.75 pw)	Reduced annuity to spouse	Depends on NICs
(ii) SERPS	60-65	National Insurance	None	25% x revalued earnings (Reduces to 20% from 2010 phased in from 1999/00 at ½% per year)	Spouse inherits entitlement	• Govt incentive to contract out 4.6% max 25% of average earnings. • SERPS Death Benefit → 50% in 2000.
2. OCCUPATIONAL (Benefits depend on particular scheme rules, but subject to Inland Revenue maxima)	60-75	15% × remuneration (Including AVCs and FSAVCs)	Final salary × 3/80 × no of years service (max 1.5 × final pay) The maximum is: 1.5 × £90,600 = £135,900	final salary 1/60 × no of years service (max 2/3 final pay) The maximum is: 2/3 × 90,600 = 60,400	Before retirement 4 × annual salary max plus dependant's pension After retirement 2/3 × pension to widow	(i) Defined benefits depends on final salary. (ii) Defined contribution depends on amount paid into pension. No carry forward/back
3. PERSONAL	50-75	Age related (% given in exam)	Maximum 25% of fund amount	Unlimited	5% of NRE cover	(i) Ideal for self employed (ii) Unused relief can be carried forward for 7 years

Notes

(i) Retirement Annuity Plans are the predecessor (Pre July 1988) to PPPs
(ii) If a lump sum is taken, then the annuity amount reduces.
(iii) Widow's pension is 2/3 of anticipated pension.
(iv) Cap of £90,600 applies to contributions and benefits for occupational schemes, just contributions for personal pensions
(v) Max number of years service = 40 (or 45).
(vi) State pension age will be 65 for all from 2020 (phased in from 2010).

3 COMPARING AND CONTRASTING COMPANY PENSION SCHEMES AND PERSONAL PENSION PLANS

		Company scheme	Personal scheme
3.1	Contributions	The employer has to contribute.	Employer has no obligation, but if does then reduces contribution limits.
3.2	Retirement date	May be able to retire and get good pension if through ill-health or redundancy. Usually between 60 and 75.	If contracted out, the SERPS part can only be collected at 60. The rest can be paid from age 50, but will be much reduced if taken early.
3.3	Family protection	Usually provides cover for death in service, ill-health and death after retirement.	Death in service cover depends entirely on the amount of money in the plan at time of death. Life insurance costs are extra.
3.4	Job-changing	**Final salary.** Can be hit by job-changing because transfer value may be lower than expected and if left behind could be based on leaving salary. May be a problem if under two years' pensionable service. **Money purchase.** No problem on job-change because employee can take a transfer value.	No problem on job-change because pension is not linked to the job.
3.5	Pension level	**Final salary.** Retirement pension linked to final salary. **Money purchase.** Pension linked to fund's investment performance.	Pension linked to fund's investment performance. $\therefore$ like money purchase.
3.6	Extra years' services	Credit for 5 years (ie total 45 years max) service post the Normal Retirement Date can be obtained (if a pre '87 member). A post '87 member may only get 40 years service.	Depends on fund only. The annuity and lump sum can be drawn after retirement. Also 'phased benefits' are available.

4 COMPARISON BETWEEN RAPs AND PPPs

	RAP (Pre 30/6/88)	PPP
Benefit ages	60 - 75	50 - 75
Tax free lump sum	3 × annuity remaining after lump sum taken	25% × fund
Cash limit	£150,000	X
C/F & C/back	✓	✓
Waiver of premiums (life)	✓	✓
Contract-out facility	X	✓
Tax relief on contributions at source	X	✓ for employed not self-employed
Transfers	✓	✓
Employer's contributions	X	✓
Write in trust	✓	✓
Earnings cap	X	£91,800

5　SUMMARY OF THE OTHER SCHEMES

Occupational schemes

EXECUTIVE
- Secrecy
- Money purchase scheme for individuals
- Subject to normal EPS rules

SSAS
- < 12 members
- Directors control
- Loans to company, 50% of fund after 2 years
- Pensioneer trustee required

FURBS
- Extra above Cap
- All proceeds can be taken as a lump sum
- Benefit in kind for employee
- Business expense for employer

Self-employed/non-pensionable schemes

GROUP PPP
- Collection of individual policies
- Employer subsidises administration costs

SIPP
- Sophisticated investor
- Property/shares etc.
- Subject to PPP rules otherwise

6　CONTRACTING OUT

6.1　Contracting out of SERPS means that you are willing to forgo the benefits in return for a potential increased benefit due to growth.

The table below sets out the avenues available to contract out.

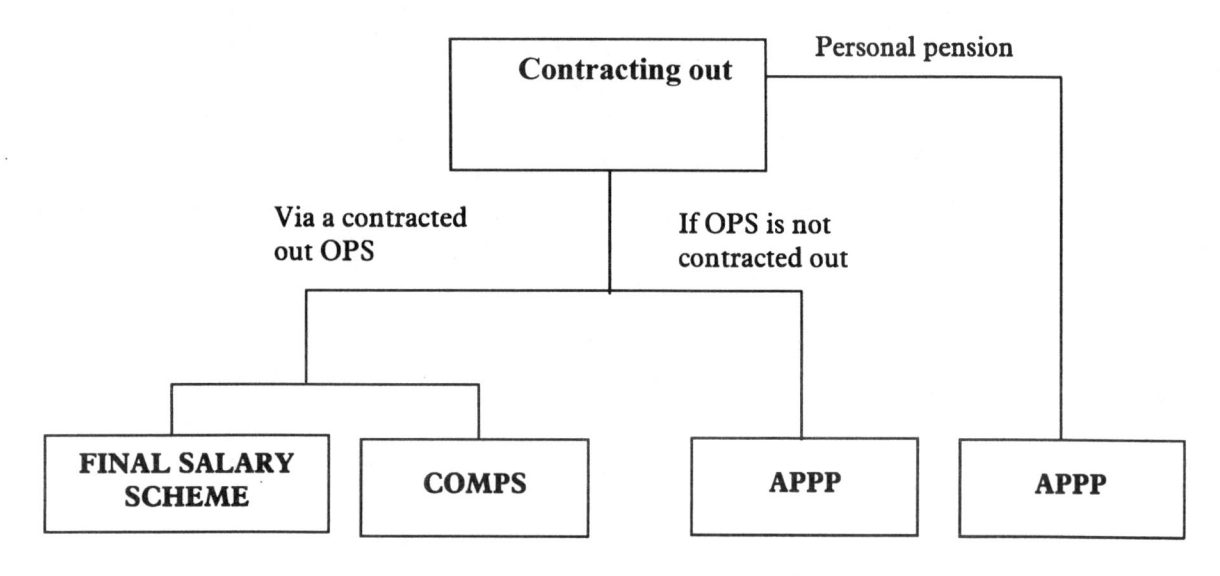

```
                        Contracting out ──────────── Personal pension
                       /       │        \
        Via a contracted       │         If OPS is not
        out OPS                │         contracted out
           /    \              │              \
```

FINAL SALARY SCHEME	COMPS	APPP	APPP
• GMP (pre 1997) • Protected rights • Reduced NICs (A reference scheme test is now used in place of GMP)	• Protected rights • Age related rebates (LOWER than APPP) • Reduced NIC	• Protected rights • Age related rebates of NIC • No reduction in NICs when paid	• Protected rights • Age related rebates of NIC • No reduction in NIC when paid

Tax Relief on Contributions

6.2

		Investor's payment	Fund reclaim	Pension contribution	Tax reduction by assessment/ payslip
Self employed					
PPP or RAC pay gross					
	- BRT	100 gross	-	100	(22)
	- HRT	100 gross	-	100	(40)
Employed - OPS					
Normal or AVC	- BRT	100 gross		100	(22)
	- HRT	100 gross		100	(40)
FSAVC	- BRT	78 net	22	100	
	- HRT	78 net	22	100	(18)
PPP					
	- BRT	78 net	22	100	
	- HRT	78 net	22	100	(18)

Note. The self employed get tax relief on assessment. The employed will get tax relief either directly (if in an OPS) through their monthly pay check, or will pay net of 22% tax if paying into a PPP or FSAVC. Higher rate relief is given via their tax assessment where appropriate.

Section C
Mock exams

FINANCIAL PLANNING CERTIFICATE

PAPER 3

MOCK EXAM 1

FINANCIAL PLANNING CERTIFICATE
PAPER 3 - IDENTIFYING AND SATISFYING CLIENT NEEDS

SPECIAL NOTICE

All questions in this paper are based on English law and practice applicable in the 2000/01 tax year, unless stated otherwise, and should be answered accordingly.

INSTRUCTIONS

- Three hours are allowed for this paper.

- READ THE INSTRUCTIONS OVERLEAF CAREFULLY BEFORE ANSWERING ANY QUESTIONS.

The question paper consists of **three** questions. You should answer **ALL** questions. Read the questions and information provided carefully. The time allowed for the examination is 3 hours. You are advised to spend approximately 55 minutes on question 1, 70 minutes on question 2 and 55 minutes on question 3. You are strongly advised to attempt **ALL** parts of each question in order to gain maximum possible marks for each question. The number of marks allocated to each question part is given next to the question.

You have been provided with a **Product List** which you should use in answering **questions 2 and 3.** You may also find it helpful to use the **tax guides** in answering all questions.

It is important to show all steps in a calculation, even if you have used a calculator.

Question 1

You are authorised and qualified to give advice and conduct business under the Financial Services Act.

Client information

James Stewart is 47 and in good health. With his wife Carol (age 39), he runs a small business involved with the distribution of specialist air filters to the automotive industry.

Mr Stewart draws an income of £13,000 per annum from the business. Mrs Stewart is paid a monthly salary from the business of £300 and she tells you that she pays no income tax or National Insurance Contributions on this income.

Mr and Mrs Stewart have two children, the youngest is 8 years old and the oldest is aged 14. The Stewart family live in a large farmhouse valued at £175,000.

Mr Stewart tells you they have an endowment mortgage taken out when they moved from to their current house in April 1998 at a set rate of 6.8% for three years. They tell you that payments increased recently following an interest rate change.

You are advised that the Stewarts intend to repay their mortgage in 21 years time using the maturity value of a joint life second death low cost endowment policy with Reliable Mutual who have a good with profits track record. This is guaranteed to repay the mortgage on its maturity

No start has been made on pension provision and James Stewart feels that this is an area of considerable priority. He would like to gradually scale down his activities from age 60 and finally retire at age 65. Then they would both like a cruise on the QE2.

Some years ago the Stewarts took out a unit linked whole of life policy with Amiable Life with the intention of using its maturity value in 2002, when Mrs Stewart's aunt will celebrate her 90th birthday, to pay for a family trip to visit her in South Africa.

With the financial demands of a large mortgage and the outgoings connected with their family, the Stewarts say that they do not have a great deal of 'surplus' income on a month to month basis.

They do however manage to save £100 per month in a joint account with the Devonshire Building Society and have accumulated some £8,000 by saving in this way. They see this as their 'emergency fund' and do not wish to take any risks with it; their house is old and it is only a matter of time before the roof will need to be replaced.

The Stewarts have recently had the difficult task of dealing with the estate of Mrs Stewart's late grandmother. Mrs Stewart is the sole beneficiary.

The late grandmother's house in Suffolk has now been sold and Mrs Stewart inherited a total of £40,000 in cash which has been placed on deposit in a high interest account requiring 30 days notice with the Devonshire Building Society, in Mrs Stewart's sole name.

The Stewarts will require your advice about investing their money and are concerned not only about having enough to live on in their retirement but also wish to have some money available to help either of their children later on if they should need it.

They wish to retain access to some of this money if they require it and are thinking about investing it in Government Stock through the postal service offered by the DMO because they can get tax free interest and there is no risk to their capital.

(a) From the information given note the relevant points under the headings of:

    (i) Personal and financial objectives **(10 marks)**
    (ii) Mortgage details **(5 marks)**

(b) When you review the information obtained you identify a number of possible errors or misunderstandings. List these areas of concern and indicate why the information is incomplete or incorrect. **(15 marks)**

Notes   **Mock exam 1**

(c) List the questions you will wish to ask the Stewarts before advising them in relation to their financial planning objectives. **(20 marks)**

Note: to gain maximum marks these questions must be expressed in language that the Stewarts will readily understand.

(Total marks for question: 50)

Question 2

You are authorised and qualified to give advice and conduct business under the Financial Services Act.

Client information

You have recently been to see Mr and Mrs Jones and obtained the following information.

Mr Jones will reach age 65, and retire in seven years time from his £30,000 a year job as a chemistry teacher, when he expects to need to use income from capital to supplement his anticipated pension benefits.

Mr Jones became a teacher as a second career at the age of 40 prior to which he had been employed as an industrial chemist. The teachers' pension scheme is an 80ths scheme for pension and also pays out a tax free cash sum of 3/80ths of final salary.

Mr Jones also has retained pension benefits from the occupational pension scheme of his former employer of £5,500 pa payable from age 60 which will increase at 5% pa in payment.

Mr Jones asks you for advice on the investment of £75,000 which is currently held at the Norwest Bank in an instant access account.

Mr and Mrs Jones have no dependant children and are of the view that to achieve good long term investment returns above inflation, a significant degree of risk exposure is necessary, and although they do not want to have all their money in risky investments they are willing to take a fairly aggressive investment approach.

Mrs Jones, aged 39, is a self-employed music teacher and from this earns some £7,000 each year after tax. As the Jones' are able to live quite comfortably on Mr Jones' salary she is able to save most of this income and has accumulated £25,000 which is currently invested in a National Savings Investment account. This is seen as an emergency fund to which accessibility is required.

Mrs Jones started a retirement annuity policy fifteen years ago with Amber Life and contributes £50 per month. She would like to retire in her mid 50's but, as this will be after the retirement of her husband, she wants to keep the exact timing flexible.

(a) List the factors Mr and Mrs Jones ought to take account of when they consider their sources of income after they retire and income requirements. **(6 marks)**

(b) (i) Calculate the retirement benefits payable to Mr Jones on retirement at age 65 based on his *current* salary. **(10 marks)**

    (ii) What options are open to Mr and Mrs Jones to provide for additional income benefits after retirement? **(13 marks)**

    (iii) Identify the advantages and disadvantages of each of these options. **(20 marks)**

(c) What options are open to Mr Jones in relation to the benefits from the scheme of his previous employer? **(8 marks)**

(d) Using the products list, suggest a suitable joint investment portfolio for the Jones. **(18 marks)**

(Total marks for question: 75)

Question 3

You are authorised and qualified to give advice and conduct business under the Financial Services Act.

Client information

Mrs Barnes, aged 52, has been recently widowed and has received confirmation from her late husband's employers that she will be entitled to a pension from their pension scheme of £7,500 per annum before tax.

Mrs Barnes is already in receipt of a widow's pension from the state of £320 per month and her two sons pay her £70 per week each for their 'keep'. She also has a part time job in a local newsagents that pays her £50 per week (gross).

The family home is worth approximately £60,000. The mortgage has been repaid from a mortgage protection policy that paid out immediately following Mr Barnes' death.

In 1982 Mrs Barnes effected a twenty year with profits endowment policy with the Orkney Mutual which has monthly premiums of £90. The original purpose of this policy was to fund Mr and Mrs Barnes's dream of owning a holiday home in Spain but Mrs Barnes now has no plans to move away.

Orkney Mutual has produced good results in the past but Mrs Barnes feels that she can ill afford the ongoing premiums now that her income is so much reduced. She therefore wishes to stop paying into this plan and seeks your advice on suitable options.

Last week Mrs Barnes received a cheque for £92,000 representing the death benefit from her late husband's pension scheme and she is looking to invest this to provide a regular income, but is also aware of the need to make this money last for many years and so wants to see some capital growth to protect against future inflation.

Last Saturday she had a stroke of luck and won £50,000 on the National Lottery. This is to be added to the above funds with the same overall objectives.

There are no other savings of any consequence and Mrs Barnes states that she would like to have £7,000 readily available as she is thinking of changing her car in 6 months or so time.

Mrs Barnes has little or no understanding of the stock market and is relatively cautious but accepts that some investment risk will be necessary to meet her objectives.

Having worked out carefully her expenditure in relation to her current income, she could do with another £250 per month of after tax income.

She is aware that her sons will not live at home forever and needs to be able to supplement her income at any time from her investments to meet the loss of keep money, when either or both of them decide to leave home.

(a) List the key factors that you will need to take account of in designing a suitable portfolio of investments for Mrs Barnes. **(8 marks)**

(b) (i) Using the products list provided, suggest a portfolio of investments to meet Mrs Barnes' income needs. **(18 marks)**

    (ii) Clearly show how Mrs Barnes *foreseeable* income objectives are met by this portfolio showing the correct tax treatment. **(6 marks)**

(c) (i) Identify the options available to Mrs Barnes in relation to the Orkney Mutual endowment policy. **(6 marks)**

    (ii) What are the advantages and disadvantages associated with each of these options? **(12 marks)**

(Total marks for question: 50)

PRODUCT LIST

In preparing your answers, you should use only products listed below.

1. Bank and Building Society Accounts - UK

	Gross Yield	Net Yield
Tinytown Bank Cheque Account (min £1)	1.8%	1.44%
Tinytown Bank Deposit Account (min £10)	2.6%	2.08%
Townshires Building Society Reserve (min £4,000)	5.0%	4%
Townshires Building Society 90 Day (min £10,000)	6.2%	4.96%
Tinytown Bank 60 Day Account (min £20,000)	6.0%	4.8%

2. Offshore Accounts - Channel Islands

	Gross Yield
Channel Bank Offshore Deposit Account (min £20,000)	6.2% (paid gross)
Townshires Building Society Offshore Account (min £20,000)	6.8% (paid gross)
Tinytown Bank Offshore Account (min £5,000)	6.7% (paid gross)

3. National Savings

	Gross Yield	20% Tax	40% Tax
Investment Account (£20 to £100,000) [i]	3.65%	2.88%	2.19%
Income Bond (£500 to £24,999)	4.95%	3.96%	2.376%
Income Bond (£25,000 to £1m)	5.2%	4.16%	3.12%
Capital Bond (£100 to £250,000)	4.65%	3.72%	2.79%
*Children's Bonus Bond (£25 to £1,000)	4.65%	4.65%	4.65%
*NSC 51st Issue (£100 to £10,000)	3.5%	3.5%	3.5%
*NSC 15th Index-linked (£100 to £10,000)	Inflation + 1.65%	Inflation + 1.65%	Inflation + 1.65%
Pensioner's Guaranteed Income Bond (£500 - £1m)	4.65%	3.72%	2.79%

(i) Rates range from 3.65% to 4.95% depending on balance

(* Tax free)

4. Guaranteed Income Bonds

	Guaranteed Yield (net of 20% tax)
Central Insurance 1 year Income Bond	4.8%
Solid Insurance 3 year Income Bond	5.9%
Fairplay Insurance 4 year Income Bond	6.3%
Central Insurance 5 year Income Bond	6.4%

5. Single Premium Investment Bonds

Fairplay Insurance Managed
Solid Insurance Recovery
Mutual Life Pacific
PDQ American
Central Insurance UK Growth
Mutual Life Property

6. With Profit Bond

XYZ Life With-Profits Bond
PDQ With-Profits Bond
Central With-Profits Bond

7. Annuity rates

Annual income payable monthly in advance for purchase price of £10,000

	Single Life, guaranteed five years, level	
	Male 65	Female 60
XYZ Life	£1,100	£902
Solid Insurance	£1,143	£894
Mutual Life	£1,154	£921

	Single Life, guaranteed five years, escalating 5%	
	Male 60	Female 55
XYZ Life	£681	£462
Solid Insurance	£700	£471
Mutual Life	£652	£439

	Male 65	Female 60
Fairplay Insurance	£773	£560
XYZ Life	£781	£578
Solid Insurance	£756	£565

	Joint Life, guaranteed five years monthly in advance, level	
	Male 60/ Female 55	Male 65/Female 60
XYZ Life	781	882
Solid Insurance	774	859
Mutual Life	802	850

8. Pension Funds

Fairplay Insurance Managed
Solid Pensions UK Equity
PDQ Fixed Interest
PDQ Recovery
XYZ With-Profits

9. Unit Trusts

	Gross Yield
Interglobal UK Income	3.8%
XYZ Equity Income	4.2%
Countryside UK Income	4.4%
*XYZ Gilt Fund	6.2%
*PDQ Fixed Interest	6.3%
*Solid Fixed Interest	6.6%
Interglobal UK Growth	0.9%
PDQ Recovery	1.2%
Interglobal US	-
Interglobal Japan	-
Fairplay Japan	-
Fairplay Property	2.2%
XYZ International Fund	2.1%
Mutual Property Fund	1.9%

* Invested in gilts and fixed interest securities

Notes: Both INCOME AND ACCUMULATION units are available except in the case of US and Japan funds, where only ACCUMULATION units are available

Share exchange facilities are available.

10. Investment Trusts

	Gross Yield
Montgomery UK	3.2%
Montgomery European	2.6%
Grimmett US	2.2%
Mountain Income	4.3%
Simmonds UK	3.8%

11. FSA Recognised Offshore Funds - Channel Islands

	Gross Yield (pa)	Paid
*PDQ Offshore Gilt Fund	6.1%	Monthly
*Solid Gilt Fund	6.6%	Monthly
*Mountain Gilt Fund	6.8%	Quarterly
Mountain UK Income	6.2%	Half-yearly
XYZ European Fund	3.8%	Half-yearly
Simmonds UK Offshore Fund	5.3%	Half-yearly

Gross but taxable yield payable to UK residents

*Invested in gilts and fixed interest deposits

12. Maxi – ISA's

	Gross Yield
Interglobal Income	4.2%
Interglobal Growth	3.1%
XYZ Europe	3.6%
XYZ Environment Fund	3.8%
Solid UK	4.1%
XYZ High Income	5.2%
Specialised Utilities	6.1%

13. INCOME TAX

TAX RATES	2000/01	1999/00
Starting rate	10%	10%
Basic rate	22%	23%
Higher rate	40%	40%
Starting rate payable on income up to	£1,520	£1,500
Higher rate payable on income over	£28,400	£28,000

MAIN PERSONAL RELIEFS	2000/01 £	1999/00 £
Personal allowance	4,385	4,335
Registered blind persons allowance	1,400	1,330

AGE ALLOWANCE

	2000/01	1999/00
Aged 65-74:		
Personal allowance	5,790	5,720
Married couple's allowance*	5,185	5,125
Aged 75 and over:		
Personal allowance	6,050	5,980
Married couple's allowance*	5,255	5,195

Limited to 10% (for 2000/01) Must be 65 before 6 April 2000

14. INHERITANCE TAX

RATES OF TAX APPLICABLE ON DEATH

Estate value	Rate
Up to £234,000	Nil
Excess over £234,000	40% of excess

EXEMPTIONS

		£
Inter spouse transfers (UK domiciled spouse)		No limit
Inter spouse transfers (non-UK domiciled spouse)	(cumulative)	55,000
Gifts to UK registered charities		No limit

Lifetime transfers
- Annual exemption per donor — 3,000
- Small gifts, annual amount per donee — 250
  (note that this cannot be used to cover part of a larger gift)

Normal expenditure — Depends on circumstances

Gifts in consideration of marriage
- By a parent — 5,000
- By a grandparent — 2,500
- By bride or groom (to groom or bride respectively) — 2,500
- By any other person — 1,000

15. CAPITAL GAINS TAX

RATES OF TAX

For individuals, chargeable gains, after deduction of allowable losses, are taxable at the income tax rates which would apply if the gains were treated as extra income.

In the case of trustees of all types of trusts, the rate is 34%.

Tapering relief will apply to assets disposed of after 6th April 1998. The amount of relief will depend upon the length of time the asset is held from 6th April 1998. Assets must be held for more than 3 years for tapering relief to apply.

INDEXATION

In calculating the chargeable gain, the purchase price can be adjusted to allow for inflation as measured by the RPI. In the case of assets purchased on or before 31 March 1982, the value of the asset on 31 March 1982 is normally used, and is adjusted by the increase in RPI since that date.

In general it follows that only gains made since 31 March 1982 are chargeable, although a number of exceptions apply.

For disposals on or after 6 April 1995, it is not possible to utilise indexation relief to create or increase a loss for CGT purposes.

Indexation only applies up to 5th April 1998. Assets disposed of after this date will only be indexed up to 5th April 1998.

ANNUAL EXEMPTION

For individuals, the annual exemption for 2000/01 is £7,200, which applies individually to husband and wife.

For trusts, the exemption in most cases is £3,600.

CHATTELS EXEMPTION

Gains on chattels where the proceeds are no more than £6,000 per item are wholly exempt.

In some cases, a measure of relief may be available where the proceeds of a sale are between £6,000 and £15,000.

PENSION CONTRIBUTIONS

The table below shows the maximum allowable contribution to Personal Pension Schemes or Retirement Annuity Contracts, expressed as a percentage of Net Relevant Earnings.

Age on 6 April	Personal Pension Schemes	Retirement Annuity Contracts
Up to 35	17.5 %	17.5 %
36-45	20.0 %	17.5 %
46-50	25.0 %	17.5 %
51-55	30.0 %	20.0 %
56-60	35.0 %	22.5 %
61-74	40.0 %	27.5 %

FINANCIAL PLANNING CERTIFICATE

PAPER 3

MOCK EXAM 2

FINANCIAL PLANNING CERTIFICATE
PAPER 3 - IDENTIFYING AND SATISFYING CLIENT NEEDS

SPECIAL NOTICE

All questions in this paper are based on English law and practice applicable in the 2000/01 tax year, unless stated otherwise, and should be answered accordingly.

INSTRUCTIONS

- Three hours are allowed for this paper.
- READ THE INSTRUCTIONS OVERLEAF CAREFULLY BEFORE ANSWERING ANY QUESTIONS.

The question paper consists of **three** questions. You should answer **ALL** questions. Read the questions and information provided carefully. The time allowed for the examination is 3 hours. You are advised to spend approximately 55 minutes on question 1, 70 minutes on question 2 and 55 minutes on question 3. You are strongly advised to attempt **ALL** parts of each question in order to gain maximum possible marks for each question. The number of marks allocated to each question part is given next to the question.

You have been provided with a **Product List** which you should use in answering **questions 2 and 3**. You may also find it helpful to use the **tax guides** in answering all questions.

It is important to show all steps in a calculation, even if you have used a calculator.

Question 1

You are authorised and qualified to give advice and conduct business under the Financial Services Act.

Client information

Charles Beaumont is aged 55 (in 2000) and is employed by Security Alarms Ltd with a salary of £40,000.

Charles tells you that he has been a member of the company pension scheme since he joined Security Alarms Ltd in 1990, and so will have twenty years of service to count towards his pension when he retires at the scheme retirement age of 60.

Charles tells you the pension scheme gives a sixtieth of final pensionable salary in respect of each year of membership together with a tax free lump sum of 1.5 times his final earnings.

Charles is concerned about having sufficient income to live on when he retires and now that his three children have grown up and left home, he has income to spare of around £300 per month which accumulates in his Bank current account.

Periodically Charles transfers excess funds from his current account to an Instant Access account at the Norstar Building Society. This account has a balance now of £12,000.

Eunice, Charles's wife, is aged 47 and has her own business running a delicatessen. As Eunice originally comes from Australia, the Beaumonts are planning a trip to see her family in Perth in three years' time, and have been saving up to do this with an endowment policy taken out with Alliance Mutual five years ago.

The business now only makes a very small profit and Eunice only wishes to draw enough to pay some of the domestic bills and the £300 per month personal pension plan contributions she started five years ago. She would like to sell the business at the same time as when Charles retires so they can spend more time together.

Mr and Mrs Beaumont tell you that their £20,000 endowment mortgage is due to finish in four years time but they will repay it early if they can afford to do so.

(a) Summarise in note form the relevant information under the headings of:

    (i) Pension details **(7 marks)**
    (ii) Future objectives relevant to financial planning **(7 marks)**

(b) Identify and describe any apparent errors or inconsistencies in the information you have been given. **(18 marks)**

(c) In suitable language identify the questions you would wish to ask of Mr and Mrs Beaumont to clarify the information you have so you can provide recommendations relevant to their objectives. **(18 marks)**

(Total marks for question: 50)

Note: to gain maximum marks these questions must be expressed in language that the Beaumonts will readily understand.

Question 2

You are authorised and qualified to give advice and conduct business under the Financial Services Act.

Client information

Mr Bennett is aged 48 and is a self-employed painter and decorator. He and his wife Amy, aged 32, have two children, Emma aged 13 and David who is 10.

The Bennett family live in a council house which they could now buy at a discounted price of £27,000 whereas the full value of the house is estimated at £45,000. They currently pay rent of £65 per week.

Until three years ago Mr Bennett was employed by a local building firm but he then decided to start his own business. Mr Bennett's accountant has advised him that his net relevant earnings for the 2000/01 tax year will be some £17,000, and were £15,000 for 1999/00.

Mr Bennett has a relatively cautious approach to investment risk and would like to be able to retire by the age of 60. Mr and Mrs Bennett have managed to save £7,000 in the Building Society which they regard as their 'emergency fund'.

Mr Bennett is concerned about the amount of income tax he will be liable to pay and is also concerned about the need to make adequate pension provision.

As his former employer did not operate any form of pension scheme, Mr Bennett took out his own personal pension over six years ago and has managed to keep this going by paying a monthly contribution of £80. Mr Bennett would like to retire by the age of 65.

The Bennetts have inherited £55,000 following the death of Mrs Bennett's mother. Mr and Mrs Bennett have agreed that they should use all of this unexpected windfall towards making provision for income on the retirement of Mr Bennett.

Mr Bennett has no existing life assurance cover but took out a sickness policy two years ago which provides for an annual income of £12,000 payable after a waiting period of 13 weeks. Now that business seems to be improving he would like to review the cover provided by this policy and also wants to know how best to provide for life insurance to protect his family.

(a) (i) In your review of Mr Bennett's sickness insurance, what factors may influence your advice? **(10 marks)**

(ii) Identify the options available to Mr Bennett to provide for life insurance cover to protect his family. **(10 marks)**

(iii) Which life insurance option would you regard as being the most suitable and why? **(7 marks)**

(b) (i) Mr Bennett wants to make proper provision for his retirement. Before advising him further, identify any further information or clarification you would require. **(14 marks)**

(ii) Calculate the maximum personal pension contribution that Mr Bennett could now make, excluding carry forwards and any options with regard to those contributions.

Show all your workings. **(10 marks)**

(c) Given Mr Bennett's stated objectives, outline a suitable portfolio of investment products to meet his retirement provision requirements. **(14 marks)**

(d) What factors should Mr and Mrs Bennett take into account in deciding whether they should take up the opportunity of buying the house? **(10 marks)**

(Total marks for question: 75)

Question 3

You are authorised and qualified to give advice and conduct business under the Financial Services Act.

Client information

Mr and Mrs Green are aged 72 and 59 respectively. Mr Green is receiving a fixed pension from his former employer's pension scheme of £1,800 pa. Mr Green had left his former employer in 1977 on being made redundant, and from that time was self employed as a surveyor until his retirement at the age of 65.

Mrs Green has never worked and the Greens' only additional income is from Mr Green's total state pension of some £5,611 per year (single person's and dependant's pension).

The Greens' home is worth some £120,000 and there is no mortgage on the property.

Until he retired, Mr Green's business was quite successful and over the years he accumulated money in a Moneywise Building Society Instant Access Account which is now has a balance of £125,000 and earns 4% gross, in his name.

The Greens have no dependants, but are finding it increasingly difficult to make ends meet. They tell you that they would like to increase after tax savings income to £600 per month without undue overall risk to their capital.

The Greens have no other investments and they have a cautious attitude to investment risk but are concerned that their future income should be able to keep pace with inflation.

The Greens have decided that on the second death they want their estate to go to charity.

(a) List the factors that will influence you in the design of a suitable investment portfolio for Mr and Mrs Green. **(6 marks)**

(b) (i) Using the tax tables calculate the Greens' current after tax income. **(10 marks)**

    (ii) What matters relating to tax will be relevant in the design of a suitable investment portfolio for the Greens. **(6 marks)**

    (iii) Using the product list provided design a suitable portfolio to meet the Greens' stated needs, showing how the required income will be provided. **(16 marks)**

(c) For each product selected give clear and concise reasons for your recommendation.
(12 marks)

(Total marks for question: 50)

PRODUCT LIST

In preparing your answers, you should use only products listed below.

1. Bank and Building Society Accounts - UK

	Gross Yield	Net Yield
Tinytown Bank Cheque Account (min £1)	1.8%	1.44%
Tinytown Bank Deposit Account (min £10)	2.6%	2.08%
Townshires Building Society Reserve (min £4,000)	5.0%	4%
Townshires Building Society 90 Day (min £10,000)	6.2%	4.96%
Tinytown Bank 60 Day Account (min £20,000)	6.0%	4.8%

2. Offshore Accounts - Channel Islands

	Gross Yield
Channel Bank Offshore Deposit Account (min £20,000)	6.2% (paid gross)
Townshires Building Society Offshore Account (min £20,000)	6.8% (paid gross)
Tinytown Bank Offshore Account (min £5,000)	6.7% (paid gross)

3. National Savings

	Gross Yield	20% Tax	40% Tax
Investment Account (£20 to £100,000) [i]	3.65%	2.88%	2.19%
Income Bond (£500 to £24,999)	4.95%	3.96%	2.376%
Income Bond (£25,000 to £1m)	5.2%	4.16%	3.12%
Capital Bond (£100 to £250,000)	4.65%	3.72%	2.79%
*Children's Bonus Bond (£25 to £1,000)	4.65%	4.65%	4.65%
*NSC 51st Issue (£100 to £10,000)	3.5%	3.5%	3.5%
*NSC 15th Index-linked (£100 to £10,000)	Inflation + 1.65%	Inflation + 1.65%	Inflation + 1.65%
Pensioner's Guaranteed Income Bond (£500 - £1m)	4.65%	3.72%	2.79%

(i) Rates range from 3.65% to 4.95% depending on balance

(* Tax free)

4. Guaranteed Income Bonds

	Guaranteed Yield (net of 20% tax)
Central Insurance 1 year Income Bond	4.8%
Solid Insurance 3 year Income Bond	5.9%
Fairplay Insurance 4 year Income Bond	6.3%
Central Insurance 5 year Income Bond	6.4%

5. **Single Premium Investment Bonds**

Fairplay Insurance Managed
Solid Insurance Recovery
Mutual Life Pacific
PDQ American
Central Insurance UK Growth
Mutual Life Property

6. **With Profit bond**

XYZ Life With-Profits Bond
PDQ With-Profits Bond
Central With-Profits Bond

7. **Annuity rates**

Annual Income payable monthly in advance for purchase price of £10,000

	Single Life, guaranteed five years, level	
	Male 65	Female 60
XYZ Life	£1,100	£902
Solid Insurance	£1,143	£894
Mutual Life	£1,154	£921

	Single Life, guaranteed five years, escalating 5%	
	Male 60	Female 55
XYZ Life	£681	£462
Solid Insurance	£700	£471
Mutual Life	£652	£439
	Male 65	Female 60
Fairplay Insurance	£773	£560
XYZ Life	£781	£578
Solid Insurance	£756	£565

	Joint Life, guaranteed five years monthly in advance, level	
	Male 60/ Female 55	Male 65/Female 60
XYZ Life	781	882
Solid Insurance	774	859
Mutual Life	802	850

8. Pension Funds

Fairplay Insurance Managed
Solid Pensions UK Equity
PDQ Fixed Interest
PDQ Recovery
XYZ With-Profits

9. Unit Trusts

	Gross Yield
Interglobal UK Income	3.8%
XYZ Equity Income	4.2%
Countryside UK Income	4.4%
*XYZ Gilt Fund	6.2%
*PDQ Fixed Interest	6.3%
*Solid Fixed Interest	6.6%
Interglobal UK Growth	0.9%
PDQ Recovery	1.2%
Interglobal US	-
Interglobal Japan	-
Fairplay Japan	-
Fairplay Property	2.2%
XYZ International Fund	2.1%
Mutual Property Fund	1.9%

* Invested in gilts and fixed interest securities

Notes: Both INCOME AND ACCUMULATION units are available except in the case of US and Japan funds, where only ACCUMULATION units are available

- Share exchange facilities are available.

10. Investment Trusts

	Gross Yield
Montgomery UK	3.2%
Montgomery European	2.6%
Grimmett US	2.2%
Mountain Income	4.3%
Simmonds UK	3.8%

11. FSA Recognised Offshore Funds - Channel Islands

	Gross Yield (pa)	Paid
*PDQ Offshore Gilt Fund	6.1%	Monthly
*Solid Gilt Fund	6.6%	Monthly
*Mountain Gilt Fund	6.8%	Quarterly
Mountain UK Income	6.2%	Half-yearly
XYZ European Fund	3.8%	Half-yearly
Simmonds UK Offshore Fund	5.3%	Half-yearly

Gross but taxable yield payable to UK residents

*Invested in gilts and fixed interest deposits

12. Maxi – ISA's

	Gross Yield
Interglobal Income	4.2%
Interglobal Growth	3.1%
XYZ Europe	3.6%
XYZ Environment Fund	3.8%
Solid UK	4.1%
XYZ High Income	5.2%
Specialised Utilities	6.1%

13. INCOME TAX

TAX RATES	2000/01	1999/00
Starting rate	10%	10%
Basic rate	22%	23%
Higher rate	40%	40%
Starting rate payable on income up to	£1,520	£1,500
Higher rate payable on income over	£28,400	£28,000

MAIN PERSONAL RELIEFS	2000/01 £	1999/00 £
Personal allowance	4,385	4,335
Registered blind persons allowance	1,400	1,330

AGE ALLOWANCE

	2000/01	1999/00
Aged 65-74:		
Personal allowance	5,790	5,720
Married couple's allowance*	5,185	5,125
Aged 75 and over:		
Personal allowance	6,050	5,980
Married couple's allowance*	5,255	5,195

Limited to 10% for (2000/01) must be 65 before 6 April 2000

14. INHERITANCE TAX

RATES OF TAX APPLICABLE ON DEATH

Estate value	Rate
Up to £234,000	Nil
Excess over £234,000	40% of excess

EXEMPTIONS

		£
Inter spouse transfers (UK domiciled spouse)		No limit
Inter spouse transfers (non-UK domiciled spouse)	(cumulative)	55,000
Gifts to UK registered charities		No limit

Lifetime transfers:
- annual exemption per donor — 3,000
- small gifts, annual amount per donee — 250
  (note that this cannot be used to cover part of a larger gift)

Normal expenditure — Depends on circumstances

Gifts in consideration of marriage:
- by a parent — 5,000
- by a grandparent — 2,500
- by bride or groom (to groom or bride respectively) — 2,500
- by any other person — 1,000

15. CAPITAL GAINS TAX

RATES OF TAX

For individuals, chargeable gains, after deduction of allowable losses are taxable at the income tax rates which would apply if the gains were treated as extra income.

In the case of trustees of all types of trusts the rate is 34%.

Tapering relief will apply to assets disposed of after 6th April 1998. The amount of relief will depend upon the length of time the asset is held from 6th April 1998. Assets must be held for more than 3 years for tapering relief to apply.

INDEXATION

In calculating the chargeable gain, the purchase price can be adjusted to allow for inflation as measured by the RPI. In the case of assets purchased on or before 31 March 1982, the value of the asset on 31 March 1982 is normally used, and is adjusted by the increase in RPI since that date.

In general it follows that only gains made since 31 March 1982 are chargeable, although a number of exceptions apply.

For disposals on or after 6 April 1995, it is not possible to utilise indexation relief to create or increase a loss for CGT purposes.

Indexation only applies up to 5th April 1998. Assets disposed of after this date will only be indexed up to 5th April 1998.

ANNUAL EXEMPTION

For individuals, the annual exemption for 2000/01 is £7,200, which applies individually to husband and wife.

For trusts, the exemption in most cases is £3,600.

CHATTELS EXEMPTION

Gains on chattels where the proceeds are no more than £6,000 per item are wholly exempt.

In some cases, a measure of relief may be available where the proceeds of a sale are between £6,000 and £15,000.

PENSION CONTRIBUTIONS

The table below shows the maximum allowable contribution to Personal Pension Schemes or Retirement Annuity Contracts, expressed as a percentage of Net Relevant Earnings.

Age on 6 April	Personal Pension Schemes	Retirement Annuity Contracts
Up to 35	17.5 %	17.5 %
36-45	20.0 %	17.5 %
46-50	25.0 %	17.5 %
51-55	30.0 %	20.0 %
56-60	35.0 %	22.5 %
61-74	40.0 %	27.5 %

FINANCIAL PLANNING CERTIFICATE

PAPER 3

MOCK EXAM 3

FINANCIAL PLANNING CERTIFICATE
PAPER 3 - IDENTIFYING AND SATISFYING CLIENT NEEDS

SPECIAL NOTICE

All questions in this paper are based on English law and practice applicable in the 2000/01 tax year, unless stated otherwise, and should be answered accordingly.

INSTRUCTIONS

- Three hours are allowed for this paper.

- READ THE INSTRUCTIONS OVERLEAF CAREFULLY BEFORE ANSWERING ANY QUESTIONS.

The question paper consists of **three** questions. You should answer **ALL** questions. Read the questions and information provided carefully. The time allowed for the examination is 3 hours. You are advised to spend approximately 55 minutes on question 1, 70 minutes on question 2 and 55 minutes on question 3. You are strongly advised to attempt **ALL** parts of each question in order to gain maximum possible marks for each question. The number of marks allocated to each question part is given next to the question.

You have been provided with a **Product List** which you should use in answering **questions 2 and 3**. You may also find it helpful to use the **tax guides** in answering all questions.

It is important to show all steps in a calculation, even if you have used a calculator.

Question 1

You are authorised and qualified to give advice and conduct business under the Financial Services Act.

John Davison is aged 43. He is married to Brenda who is 45 years of age. John is employed by a well known DIY Group. He has worked for them for the last 22 years and is now the manager of a new superstore which has opened recently.

John was promoted to this important position after several years of working his way up the company. This has meant that the Davisons have had to move house 4 times as Mr Davison's working location has changed and he is about to move again to be near to the new store.

John is very highly regarded by his employer. He feels that he has deserved this new job and that it puts him nicely in line for promotion when the area manager retires in 2 years time.

Brenda has been a little put out by the number of house moves that they have had to make but she has supported John in his career and she is pleased that he now seems to have achieved an important position. Brenda is looking forward to moving as they are returning to where they used to live when they first married and where their family and a number of friends still live.

Brenda and John have twin children, Brian and Jenny, who are 21 and have both left home to share a flat together in town.

John and Brenda are both members of the local health club and enjoy walking and cycling. They also enjoy travelling and make sure that they have a holiday each year. They usually go to the Canary Islands where they stay in a friend's villa. However, they also like to have a winter holiday every 3/4 years to 'somewhere special'. The whole family went to Tobago last January, and John had to use all of his £5,000 overdraft facility to help with the total cost of around £6,500. Brenda and John have agreed that their next holiday will be 3 weeks in Australia, hopefully in 3 years' time.

Brenda enjoys writing short stories and often gets them published in magazines. This brings in around £450 per month, most of which she manages to save, although she does enjoy the element of financial independence that the cash gives her.

John earns £35,000 and his main concern is raising the finance to purchase their new home. They expect to raise £120,000 from the sale of their existing house. The new house will only cost them £80,000 to buy because it is in need of a lot of modernisation work. They have been told by a local builder that the work will cost them a further £50,000 to carry out. John and Brenda are happy with this since the house is in a nice location and they estimate that it will be worth about £175,000 when the work is complete.

They have an existing mortgage of £40,000 which costs them £275 a month and John and Brenda are keen to maintain their outlay as close to this figure as possible. Brenda is especially concerned that the new mortgage does not exceed the £60,000 limit for tax relief. She feels that as John has to pay 40% tax on all of his income, they should get as much of this back as they can.

John's family are covered by the firm's private medical insurance scheme although Brenda hopes that their family's health stays as good as it is right now and they never have to make a claim. In addition, John is a member of the company pension scheme which is a 60ths scheme. He is looking forward to receiving a 2/3rds pension when he retires at age 65 on top of the tax-free lump sum of 1.5 times his salary. He would like to retire earlier if he can and has mentioned the possibility of going in 15 years time when he will be 58.

John has a private permanent health insurance policy for the maximum allowed (66%), which he took out 2 years ago and, in addition they have an endowment plan with Reliable Life. This plan costs them £60 per month but they are just about to surrender it because it relates to the mortgage on the house they are now selling. They do not have any HP or credit and they pay off the balance on their Visa card each month.

John and Brenda have no life cover apart from the cover provided by John's employer. John is not sure how much cover there is but he thinks that a figure of twice his salary rings a bell. Brenda is certain that the amount of cover is 6 times John's salary, a total of £180,000.

John has an endowment savings plan which he took out when he was 20. He pays £10 per month and it is due to mature when he is 50. He has been told that it should be worth about £22,000. Brenda saved £30 per month into a PEP Savings Plan until April 1999. She took this out 2 years ago in 1997 after reading in the *Sunday Times* about the opportunities that exist in emerging markets. She believes that it is currently worth about £3,000.

John's father died last year and left them £25,000 plus some money for the children which they received on their 21st birthday. The £25,000 is in their joint bank account.

A solicitor drew up a will for them both shortly after John's father died.

They are aware that they may need financial advice in a number of areas but they have not yet prioritised these in any way.

(a) From the information provided by Mr and Mrs Davison, please provide, **in note form**, the relevant points under the following headings.

    (i) Personal details   **(10 marks)**

    (ii) Financial details   **(8 marks)**

    (iii) Pension details   **(3 marks)**

    (iv) Financial objectives   **(3 marks)**

    (v) Calculate the maximum weekly benefit that John Davison would be able to claim from his PHI policy.   **(3 marks)**

(Total 27 marks)

(b) From the information supplied, please identify and describe, in note form, any inconsistencies and/or apparent errors that appear.   **(10 marks)**

(c) Please write down, in note form, a list of questions that you would need to ask Mr and Mrs Davison in order to provide you with the information required to confirm their existing income and expenditure arrangements.   **(13 marks)**

(Total marks for question: 50)

Question 2

You are authorised to give advice and conduct business under the Financial Services Act.

At the age of 44, Dennis Allen is beginning to think about his retirement and his situation regarding a pension. He is currently employed on a salary of £19,000 a year. He does not receive any benefits-in-kind nor any overtime/bonus payments. He is not a member of an occupational pension scheme but he does currently contribute £80 per month net into a personal pension. The present value of this plan is £27,500 which includes £5,250 in respect of protected rights, reflecting the fact that he has contracted out of SERPS.

Dennis has £750 in a Gold Account with the Town Building Society which he regards as his emergency fund, although he does not think that it is sufficient for this purpose. He also has savings of £3,500 which he keeps separately in a different Gold Account at the same building society.

His wife, Belinda (40) has just returned to full time work. She earns a salary of £7,500 and has no pension plan, either from her employer or personally.

Dennis's father died last year and left them £35,000 which is currently in a deposit account at their bank. They feel that they would be able to commit some of this money to longer term investments.

After taking into account their income and expenditure, the Allens believe that they can comfortably afford to save £350 per month especially now that Belinda is working full time.

You have calculated that, using carry back and carry forward provisions, Dennis has unused relief amounting to £21,000 at the end of the current tax year.

Belinda and Dennis have no other investments apart from the bank and building society deposits and Dennis has said that he likes to have as much control as possible over their financial arrangements and that he would like any investments they make to be as tax efficient as possible.

(a) List, in note form, the factors that Dennis and Belinda should take into account when considering their pension requirements. **(19 marks)**

(b) Where appropriate, use the product list provided.

    (i) Calculate the maximum gross and net single contribution that Dennis would be allowed to make into a personal pension in the current year. Show your workings. **(8 marks)**

    (ii) Design a portfolio of investment products (including an investment into a personal pension) that meets the needs of Mr and Mrs Allen. Show the amounts you recommend be invested in each contract. **(14 marks)**

(c) For each of the products you have recommended:

    (i) Justify the reasons for your recommendation **(15 marks)**

    (ii) Justify the reasons for the amounts you have recommended for each product **(6 marks)**

    (iii) Explain, in note form, your recommendations for dealing with any unused tax relief. **(2 marks)**

(cont'd)

Notes **Mock exam 3**

(d) Mr and Mrs Allen state that they can afford to save £350 per month now that Belinda is back at work.

(i) What advice would you give them regarding their savings? Explain your reasons.

(8 marks)

(ii) Explain, in note form, the steps that you would take in order to keep their savings situation under review. **(3 marks)**

(Total marks for question: 75)

Question 3

You are authorised to give advice and conduct business under the Financial Services Act.

John is aged 26. He is single. He has been with his current girlfriend for 6 years and they plan to marry although they have not yet set a date.

John recently qualified as an accountant and is employed by a medium sized local firm. His annual salary is £35,000 and whilst he appreciates that he is well paid, he feels that he earns every penny. He seldom works less than 10 hours a day and he often takes work home at the weekend. He is confident that he will prosper within the firm and he has been told by the Senior Partner that there is no reason why he should not be able to become a partner after he has worked there for at least another 5 years.

He has estimated that the cost of buying into the partnership will be around £60,000 and he currently has this money available because he inherited £250,000 when his grandmother died last month.

The money is currently in a deposit account and he has plans to buy a small house for himself as well as a new car. He has earmarked £150,000 for this, leaving him a total of £100,000 to be invested. He currently has £4,000 in his current account and feels that he would like to maintain the account at this level. He took out a TESSA in December 1998 and would like to set aside funds to feed this for the remainder of the five year term. His initial deposit was £3,000, he also contributed the maximum in 1999/2000 tax year.

His primary need is for capital growth and he has told you that whilst he understands the relationship between risk and return, he does not wish to speculate too much.

John's employer provides him with a first class pension scheme and he has no other investments.

(a) (i) List the factors which you would take into account when designing an investment portfolio for John. **(6 marks)**

    (ii) Indicate which of these factors you consider to be the most important. **(2 marks)**

(b) Using the product list provided, recommend an investment portfolio for John which meets his needs. **(11 marks)**

(c) For each of the products you have recommended justify the reason for:

    (i) Your recommendation **(15 marks)**

    (ii) The amounts you have recommended for each product **(5 marks)**

(d) In outline form, describe a long term financial planning strategy that you could present to John. **(11 marks)**

(Total marks for question: 50)

PRODUCT LIST

In preparing your answers, you should use only products listed below.

1. Bank and Building Society Accounts - UK

	Gross Yield	Net Yield
Tinytown Bank Cheque Account (min £1)	1.8%	1.44%
Tinytown Bank Deposit Account (min £10)	2.6%	2.08%
Townshires Building Society Reserve (min £4,000)	5.0%	4%
Townshires Building Society 90 Day (min £10,000)	6.2%	4.96%
Tinytown Bank 60 Day Account (min £20,000)	6.0%	4.8%

2. Offshore Accounts - Channel Islands Based

	Gross Yield
Channel Bank Offshore Deposit Account (min £20,000)	6.2% (paid gross)
Townshires Building Society Offshore Account (min £20,000)	6.8% (paid gross)
Tinytown Bank Offshore Account (min £5,000)	6.7% (paid gross)

3. National Savings

	Gross Yield	20% Tax	40% Tax
Investment Account (£20 to £100,000) [i]	3.65%	2.88%	2.19%
Income Bond (£500 to £24,999)	4.95%	3.96%	2.376%
Income Bond (£25,000 to £1m)	5.2%	4.16%	3.12%
Capital Bond (£100 to £250,000)	4.65%	3.72%	2.79%
*Children's Bonus Bond (£25 to £1,000)	4.65%	4.65%	4.65%
*NSC 51st Issue (£100 to £10,000)	3.5%	3.5%	3.5%
*NSC 15th Index-linked (£100 to £10,000)	Inflation + 1.65%	Inflation + 1.65%	Inflation + 1.65%
Pensioner's Guaranteed Income Bond (£500 - £1m)	4.65%	3.72%	2.79%

(i) Rates range from 3.65% to 4.95% depending on balance

(* Tax free)

4. Guaranteed Income Bonds

	Guaranteed Yield (net of 20% tax)
Central Insurance 1 year Income Bond	4.8%
Solid Insurance 3 year Income Bond	5.9%
Fairplay Insurance 4 year Income Bond	6.3%
Central Insurance 5 year Income Bond	6.4%

5. Single Premium Investment Bonds

Fairplay Insurance Managed
Solid Insurance Recovery
Mutual Life Pacific
PDQ American
Central Insurance UK Growth
Mutual Life Property

6. With Profit bond

XYZ Life With-Profits Bond
PDQ With-Profits Bond
Central With-Profits Bond

7. Annuity rates

Annual Income payable monthly in advance for purchase price of £10,000

	Single Life, guaranteed five years, level	
	Male 65	Female 60
XYZ Life	£1,100	£902
Solid Insurance	£1,143	£894
Mutual Life	£1,154	£921

	Single Life, guaranteed five years, escalating 5%	
	Male 60	Female 55
XYZ Life	£681	£462
Solid Insurance	£700	£471
Mutual Life	£652	£439

	Male 65	Female 60
Fairplay Insurance	£773	£560
XYZ Life	£781	£578
Solid Insurance	£756	£565

	Joint Life, guaranteed five years monthly in advance level	
	Male 60/ Female 55	Male 65/Female 60
XYZ Life	781	882
Solid Insurance	774	859
Mutual Life	802	850

8. Pension Funds

Fairplay Insurance Managed
Solid Pensions UK Equity
PDQ Fixed Interest
PDQ Recovery
XYZ With-Profits

9. Unit Trusts

	Gross Yield
Interglobal UK Income	3.8%
XYZ Equity Income	4.2%
Countryside UK Income	4.4%
*XYZ Gilt Fund	6.2%
*PDQ Fixed Interest	6.3%
*Solid Fixed Interest	6.6%
Interglobal UK Growth	0.9%
PDQ Recovery	1.2%
Interglobal US	-
Interglobal Japan	-
Fairplay Japan	-
Fairplay Property	2.2%
XYZ International Fund	2.1%
Mutual Property Fund	1.9%

* Invested in gilts and fixed interest securities

Notes: Both INCOME AND ACCUMULATION units are available except in the case of US and Japan funds, where only ACCUMULATION units are available

- Share exchange facilities are available.

10. Investment Trusts

	Gross Yield
Montgomery UK	3.2%
Montgomery European	2.6%
Grimmett US	2.2%
Mountain Income	4.3%
Simmonds UK	3.8%

11. FSA Recognised Offshore Funds - Channel Islands

	Gross Yield (p.a)	Paid
*PDQ Offshore Gilt Fund	6.1%	Monthly
*Solid Gilt Fund	6.6%	Monthly
*Mountain Gilt Fund	6.8%	Quarterly
Mountain UK Income	6.2%	Half-yearly
XYZ European Fund	3.8%	Half-yearly
Simmonds UK Offshore Fund	5.3%	Half-yearly

Gross but taxable yield payable to UK residents

*Invested in gilts and fixed interest deposits

12. Maxi – ISA's

	Gross Yield
Interglobal Income	4.2%
Interglobal Growth	3.1%
XYZ Europe	3.6%
XYZ Environment Fund	3.8%
Solid UK	4.1%
XYZ High Income	5.2%
Specialised Utilities	6.1%

13. INCOME TAX

TAX RATES	2000/01	1999/00
Starting rate	10%	10%
Basic rate	22%	23%
Higher rate	40%	40%
Starting rate payable on income up to	£1,520	£1,500
Higher rate payable on income over	£28,400	£28,000

MAIN PERSONAL RELIEFS	2000/01 £	1999/00 £
Personal allowance	4,385	4,335
Registered blind persons allowance	1,400	1,330

AGE ALLOWANCE

Aged 65-74:		
Personal allowance	5,790	5,720
Married couple's allowance*	5,185	5,125
Aged 75 and over:		
Personal allowance	6,050	5,980
Married couple's allowance*	5,255	5,195

* Limited to 10% for (2000/01) must be 65 before 6 April 2000

14. INHERITANCE TAX

RATES OF TAX APPLICABLE ON DEATH

Estate value	Rate
Up to £234,000	Nil
Excess over £234,000	40% of excess

EXEMPTIONS

		£
Inter spouse transfers (UK domiciled spouse)		No limit
Inter spouse transfers (non-UK domiciled spouse)	(cumulative)	55,000
Gifts to UK registered charities		No limit

Lifetime transfers

• Annual exemption per donor	3,000
• Small gifts, annual amount per donee	250

(note that this cannot be used to cover part of a larger gift)

Normal expenditure — Depends on circumstances

Gifts in consideration of marriage

• By a parent	5,000
• By a grandparent	2,500
• By bride or groom (to groom or bride respectively)	2,500
• By any other person	1,000

15. CAPITAL GAINS TAX

RATES OF TAX

For individuals, chargeable gains, after deduction of allowable losses are taxable at the income tax rates which would apply if the gains were treated as extra income.

In the case of trustees of all types of trusts the rate is 34%.

Tapering relief will apply to assets disposed of after 6th April 1998. The amount of relief will depend upon the length of time the asset is held from 6th April 1998. Assets must be held for more than 3 years for tapering relief to apply.

INDEXATION

In calculating the chargeable gain, the purchase price can be adjusted to allow for inflation as measured by the RPI. In the case of assets purchased on or before 31 March 1982, the value of the asset on 31 March 1982 is normally used, and is adjusted by the increase in RPI since that date.

In general it follows that only gains made since 31 March 1982 are chargeable, although a number of exceptions apply.

For disposals on or after 6 April 1995, it is not possible to utilise indexation relief to create or increase a loss for CGT purposes.

Indexation only applies up to 5th April 1998. Assets disposed of after this date will only be indexed up to 5th April 1998.

ANNUAL EXEMPTION

For individuals, the annual exemption for 2000/01 is £7,200, which applies individually to husband and wife.

For trusts, the exemption in most cases is £3,600.

CHATTELS EXEMPTION

Gains on chattels where the proceeds are no more than £6,000 per item are wholly exempt.

In some cases, a measure of relief may be available where the proceeds of a sale are between £6,000 and £15,000.

PENSION CONTRIBUTIONS

The table below shows the maximum allowable contribution to Personal Pension Schemes or Retirement Annuity Contracts, expressed as a percentage of Net Relevant Earnings.

Age on 6 April	Personal Pension Schemes	Retirement Annuity Contracts
Up to 35	17.5 %	17.5 %
36-45	20.0 %	17.5 %
46-50	25.0 %	17.5 %
51-55	30.0 %	20.0 %
56-60	35.0 %	22.5 %
61-74	40.0 %	27.5 %

SOLUTIONS TO
FINANCIAL PLANNING CERTIFICATE
PAPER 3
MOCK EXAM 1

Notes *Mock exam 1 solutions*

FP3 EXAM 1 - MARKING SCHEME

1 (a) (i) The Stewarts' personal and financial objectives

Pension provision is needed for James Stewart.	1
Repayment of the mortgage is due in 21 years' time.	1
James Stewart wants to scale down his activities from age 60.	1
James Stewart wants finally to retire at age 65.	1
Mr and Mrs Stewart would like to go on a cruise on QE2	1
Mr and Mrs Stewart would like to go to South Africa in 2002 when Mrs Stewart's Aunt celebrates her 90th birthday.	1
Mr and Mrs Stewart want to have enough to live on in their retirement.	1
Mr and Mrs Stewart want to be able to help any of their children later if they need it.	1
Investment of money received by Mrs Stewart from an inheritance.	1
Replace the roof when this is needed.	1
	10 marks

(ii) Mortgage details

The Stewarts have an endowment mortgage.	1
This was taken out in April 1998 at a rate of 6.8% for three years.	1
The Stewarts intend to repay their mortgage in 21 years' time.	1
The maturity value of a low cost endowment policy with Reliable Mutual will repay the mortgage.	1
Payments increased recently following an interest rate change.	1
	5 marks

(b) Errors/misunderstandings (to a maximum of 15 marks)

Mrs Stewart states that she has a monthly salary from the business of £300 but pays no income tax or National Insurance Contributions.	2
This level of income is above the lower earnings limit for National Insurance purposes.	1
So she must pay National Insurance Contributions.	1
The Stewarts tell you their mortgage was arranged in 1998 at a fixed rate of 6.8% for three years and that payments increased recently.	1
Was the increase in payments at the end of a three year discounted rate period rather than a fixed rate?	1
The Reputable Life low cost endowment policy is arranged on a joint life second death basis.	1
It is more likely to be on a first death basis.	1
The low cost endowment policy is guaranteed to repay the mortgage on its maturity.	1

Low cost endowment policies do not guarantee to repay on maturity but only in the event of death.	1
Is the policy on a non-profit or with-profits basis (in which case the statement would be correct)?	1
The Stewarts are thinking about investing money in Government Stock via the DMO Postal Service because they can get tax-free interest and there is no risk to their capital.	2
Interest is paid gross but it is taxable.	1
As the price of Government Stock rises and falls so does the value of their investment. So their capital cannot be said to be free of risk.	1
Term of mortgage. In 21 years' time Mr Stewart will be 68 but he states that he would like to retire by the age of 65.	1
The unit linked whole of life policy with Amiable Life will not have a maturity value in 2002.	1
The policy may be surrendered but the terms may be unattractive.	1
Is the policy perhaps an endowment policy?	1

(Maximum 15 marks)

(c) **Questions (to a maximum of 20 marks)**

(i) **Investments**

Mr Stewart: what is your attitude to investment risk?	1
Mrs Stewart: what is your attitude to investment risk?	1
How much of your money do you wish to keep accessible?	1
Do you wish to take income from your investment?	1
Do you have any other investments?	1

(ii) **Help for children later if they need it**

When do you think financial help may be required?	1
Are your children in or do you plan for them to go to private school?	1
If so, when and at what expected cost?	1

(iii) **Planned trip to South Africa**

How much will this cost?	1
Can I see your Policy with Amiable Life to check its terms and conditions?	1
How much are you expecting to be available from this policy in 2002?	1

(iv) Pension provision for James Stewart

How much do you wish to save/invest for your retirement?	1
What level of income will you require in your retirement?	1
Will you require to have some retirement income from age 60 and then phased in to age 65?	1
Do you have any pensions from any previous employment?	1

(v) Planned cruise on QE2

When do you plan to do this?	1
How much do you think it will cost?	1

(vi) Mortgage

You say that your mortgage was at a fixed rate of 6.8% for three years from April 1998 but that payments have increased recently following an interest rate change. Can I see your mortgage agreement?	1
Can I see your endowment policy with Reliable Mutual to check its terms and conditions?	1
How much was your mortgage for at outset?	1
What are your current monthly repayments and what were they before they changed?	1
Did your lender write to you confirming the change in payments, may I see that letter?	1
Who is your lender?	1

(vii) Replace the roof when required

When do you expect to have to do this?	1
How much will it cost?	1
How will you fund this?	1
Will you need to increase your mortgage at that time?	1

(Maximum 20 marks)

Mock exam 1 solutions

2 (a) Factors to be taken into account

How much income will be needed in retirement in total?	1
What benefits will be available from the teachers' pension scheme?	1
What benefits are available from Mr Jones former employer's scheme?	1
What state pension benefits will the Jones's be entitled to?	1
What are the estimated benefits from Mrs Jones retirement annuity?	1
Are there any other pension entitlements?	<u>1</u>
	6 marks

(b) (i) Retirement benefit

Benefits from Teacher's Pension Scheme will be 25/80ths (1) of final salary (1).	2
Based on current salary this amounts to £9,375 per annum.	1
In addition, there will be a tax free cash sum of 3/80ths × 25 final salary, ie £28,125.	2
In addition, Mr Jones has retained pension benefits from the scheme of a former employer.	1
This amounts to £5,500 from age 60 increasing at 5% per annum.	1
By age 65 this will have increased to £7,019 per annum	1
The basic state pension will also be payable.	1
Any SERPS pension will also be payable.	<u>1</u>
	10 marks

(b) (ii) The options available to Mr and Mrs Jones to provide for additional pension benefits

Mr Jones

Purchase of added years in the teachers' pension scheme	1
Teachers' pension scheme AVCs	1
Free-standing additional voluntary contributions	1
Establishing an Individual Savings Account	1
Investment of capital to supplement income later	1

Mrs Jones

Additional regular contributions to the retirement annuity	1
Single pension contributions to the retirement annuity	1
Regular contributions to a new personal pension	1
Single pension contributions to a new personal pension	1

Notes *Mock exam 1 solutions*

Use carry forward rules to take advantage of unused relief from previous years.		1
Transfer from the retirement annuity to a personal pension to enable benefits to be taken earlier than age 60.		1
Saving in an Individual Savings Account		1
Investment of capital to supplement income later		1
		13 marks

(b) (iii) **Advantages and disadvantages of options**

Mr Jones: buying added years

Advantages

Known future benefits	1
Includes dependant's pensions in the event of death	1
Index linked pension benefits	1
Tax relief on contributions	1

Disadvantages

Expensive	1
Inflexible	1

Mr Jones: in house AVC arrangement

Advantages

Tax relief on contributions	1
Lower charges, perhaps, than FSAVC	1
Tax free fund	
	1

Disadvantages

Lack of privacy	1
Limited investment choice	1
No benefit guarantees	1
Have to take benefit as income without tax free cash	1

Mr Jones: free-standing additional voluntary contribution scheme

Advantages

Portable	1
Greater investment choice	1
Choice of provider	1
Can be used to fund early retirement	1
Confidential	1
Tax relief on contributions	1

Tax free fund	1

Disadvantages

Higher cost than scheme AVC	1
Future benefits not guaranteed	1
Benefits to be taken as income	1

Mr and Mrs Jones: Individual Savings Accounts

Advantages

Fund accumulates tax free	1
Tax free income / capital can be taken	1
May invest up to £7,000 per annum each (2000/01)	1
Access possible at any time	1
No benefit limits	1

Disadvantages

Contributions not eligible for tax relief	1
Contributions limited to a total of £7,000 in 2000/01 (reducing to £5,000 thereafter)	1

Mr and Mrs Jones: investment of capital to supplement income later

Advantages

Income can be varied to take account of actual needs	1
Can manage risk exposure in light of income needs	1
Can eat into capital in later years to meet income needs	1

Disadvantages

Reliance on investment growth to enable future income needs to be met	1
Investment objectives may not be met leading to a shortfall	1
May need to eat into capital to enable income needs to be met	1

Mrs Jones: additional retirement annuity or personal pension payments

Advantages

Tax relief on contributions	1
Can make use of unused relief	1
Tax free fund growth	1
Tax free cash sum can be taken from proceeds	1

Mock exam 1 solutions

Retirement annuity can be transferred to personal pension
if tax free cash better.   1

Retirement annuity can be transferred to personal pension
if earlier benefits required than from age 60   1

Disadvantages

Pension is taxable when taken   1

Contributions limited as income is low   1

Any transfer from retirement annuity to personal pension
before age 60 may be subject to penalty   1

(Maximum of 6 marks in relation to each option - overall maximum 20 marks)

(c) **The options available to Mr Jones in relation to benefits arising out of the scheme of his previous employer**

	Marks
Leave benefits where they are, as a deferred pension	2
Transfer value into teachers' scheme.	2
Transfer value into section 32 buy out plan	2
Transfer value into personal pension	2
	8 marks

(d) **There is no single correct answer but the following is provided for guidance.**
We outline the maximum and minimum investment limits, but you must ensure the total amount for investment is allocated.

	£	Min £	Max £	Marks
Total for investment	100,000			1
BUT leave £25,000 on any deposit/high interest account(s)		25,000	25,000	1
Any higher interest deposit account		3,000	6,000	1
Single premium pension - Mrs Jones		1,000	6,400	2
NSC index linked issue(s)		5,000	10,000	1
Any 2 ISA's		7,000	14,000	1
With Profits Investment Bond(s)		10,000	15,000	1
Managed Investment Bonds		10,000	20,000	1
Equity based / Overseas Invested Bonds		10,000	20,000	1
Guaranteed Growth bonds			5,000	1
Unit/Investment Trusts- four or more growth Orientated funds		10,000	25,000	2
Maximum of £10,000 in any single fund				1
Spread across at least 4 products				1
At least £50,000 equity exposed				1
At least £60,000 in products that either become				1
• available for reinvestment within 7 years; or				
• which then may be used to provide an income				1

(Maximum 18 marks)

Mock exam 1 solutions Notes

3   (a) **Key factors that you will need to take account of in designing a suitable portfolio of investments for Mrs Barnes (to a maximum of 8 marks)**

Access to some capital for emergency purposes	1
To have £7,000 available when she needs it when she changes her car	1
To increase her after-tax income now by £250 per month	1
To increase her income in the future if either or both of her sons leave home	2
To protect her capital against future inflation.	2
For the capital to last for many years / acceptable level of risk	1
	8 marks

(b) (i) There is no single correct answer but the following list is for guidance in terms of acceptable products and gross and net income. Give 1 mark for suitable product and 1 for suitable amount (except cash).

	OK for Income £	Min £	Max £	Marks £
Total for investment		£142,000		1
Any Instant access Bank or Building Society	*	10,000	25,000	1
Any higher interest deposit account	*	5,000	10,000	1
NSC 50th/15th index linked Issue		10,000	20,000	2
Any ISA		3,000	7,000	2
NSC Income Bonds	*	5,000	25,000	2
With Profits Investment bonds or		10,000	25,000	2
Managed Investment Bonds		10,000	25,000	or 2
G'teed Income bonds	*	10,000	40,000	2
Unit/Investment Trusts - 2 or more funds	*	10,000	40,000	2
Maximum of £15,000 in any single fund				1
At least 4 suitable for income products				1
Max of £50,000 in equity based products				1

(Maximum 18 marks)

(ii)

After tax income must be correctly shown and in range £230 - £260 per month from acceptable products as marked with * Income from other products deducted for this purpose	2
Income after tax may be increased by £250 per month from acceptable products	2
Correct tax treatment for all products selected	2
	6 marks

An example model answer is given below.

	Gross income £	Tax	Net income £
Guaranteed income bond (Fairplay) £20,000 @ 6.3%	-	20% at source	1,260
NSC income bond £25,000 @ 5.2%	1,300	20% on assessment £260	1,040
High interest deposit (Townshires) £10,000 @ 6.2%	620	20% at source	496
Total per annum			2,796
Total per month			233

(c) (i) **Options available to Mrs Barnes in relation to the Orkney Mutual Endowment Policy**

- Surrender it — 1
- Make the policy paid-up which will give a reduction in the eventual maturity value. — 1
- Sell or auction the policy (Traded Endowment Policy or TEP) — 2
- Keep the policy going... — 1
  ...by planning for sufficient income to meet the premium — 1

(ii) **Advantages and disadvantages of each option (to a maximum of 12 marks)**

Policy surrender

Advantages

Cash available to invest or spend — 1

Savings on future premiums — 1

Disadvantages

Loss of life cover — 1

Possible surrender penalties — 1

Make policy paid-up

Advantages

Some degree of life cover maintained — 1

Premiums saved — 1

Disadvantage

Reduction in ultimate maturity value — 1

Less future bonuses/terminal bonus — 1

Sell/auction policy (TEP Market)

Advantages

Potential better cash value than surrender value — 1

Immediate cash available to spend/invest

Disadvantages

Loss of life cover — 1

The policy may be unsuitable for sale/auction — 1

May still not represent good value for money in relation to premiums paid — 1

Keep the policy going

Advantages

Potential cash value at maturity	1
Maintain life cover	1

Disadvantages

Have to pay premiums	1
Life cover not really needed	<u>1</u>
	12 marks

SOLUTIONS TO

FINANCIAL PLANNING CERTIFICATE

PAPER 3

MOCK EXAM 2

Notes   **Mock exam 2 solutions**

FP3 EXAM 2 - MARKING SCHEME

1 (a) (i) Pension details

Charles has been a member of the company pension scheme since 1990.	1
He expects to have 20 years service to count towards his pension.	1
The scheme retirement age is 60.	1
The scheme gives a 60th of final pensionable salary in respect of each year of Membership	1
The scheme also gives a tax free lump sum of 1.5 times his final earnings.	1
Charles is concerned about having enough income to live on when he retires.	1
Eunice pays £300 per month into a personal pension plan	1
	7 Marks

(ii) Future objectives relevant to financial planning

Sufficient retirement income	1
A planned trip to Australia in three years time	1
Early repayment of the mortgage if they can afford to do so	1
Eunice only wishes to draw enough from the business to pay some of the domestic bills and the £300 per month personal pension plan	2
Eunice would like to sell the business at the same time as Charles retires so they can spend more time together	2
	7 Marks

(b) Errors/inconsistencies (to a maximum of 18 marks)

Charles's pension

Charles says he has been a member of the company scheme since 1990 and so will have 20 years of service to count towards his pension at the scheme retirement age of 60.	2
Charles will be 60 in five years time.	1
Charles' years of service will be 15 and not 20.	1
Is the scheme retirement age 65?	1
Charles states that he will get a pension of a 60th of final salary in respect of each year of membership **and** a tax free cash sum of 1.5 times his final earnings.	2
Pension schemes are only allowed to give a maximum basic benefit of one 60th of final salary part of which may be commuted for a tax-free lump sum.	2

Mock exam 2 solutions Notes

The maximum lump sum of 1.5 times final pay depends on at least 20 years' service at retirement.	1
So, Charles's maximum lump sum will be less than this.	1
The Alliance Mutual Endowment Policy - the Beaumonts tell you the Policy was taken out five years ago yet they plan to use the 'maturity value' in three years time.	2
The minimum term for an endowment policy is ten years.	1
Was the policy taken out longer than five years ago?	1
Eunice says she is paying a pension contribution of £300 per month. Yet her business now only makes a very small profit.	2
Is she using up unused relief from previous years?	1
Are personal pension contributions being overpaid?	1
There is no mention of an endowment policy in support of the mortgage.	2

(**Maximum 18 marks**)

(c) **Further information (to a maximum of 18 marks)**

Charles, may I see the booklet relating to your company pension sScheme together with any recent benefit statements?	1
If you do not have a benefit statement may I, with your authority, approach your employer to establish the benefits to which you are entitled?	1
Does the pension scheme give a benefit of a 60th of final salary, which can be exchanged for a tax free lump sum or some lower benefit with a tax free lump sum?	2
Is retirement age under the pension scheme 60 or 65?	1
How much income will you need to live on, in today's terms, when you retire?	1
Of your 'spare' income, how much would you be willing to use to invest towards increasing your pension?	1
Eunice, may I see the accounts for the last few years relating to your business?	1
May I have contact with your accountant to review the profits you have made so as to check whether the pension contributions you are currently making are excessive?	2
How much profit does your business now make?	1
How much profit did the business used to make?	1
Eunice and Charles, how do you plan to repay the mortgage in four years time?	1
You did not mention the endowment policy in support of the mortgage. Can I see the policy document please?	1
May I see your endowment policy with Alliance Mutual?	1

Mock exam 2 solutions

Do you have a recent bonus notice I could see?	1
What is the policy's estimated value in three years time?	1
How much do you expect the trip to Australia to cost?	1

(Maximum 18 marks)

2 (a) (i) Mr Bennett's sickness insurance

Maximum permitted benefit is typically up to 67% of pre-disability income **less** single person's incapacity benefit.	2
For 2000/01, single person's incapacity benefit is £67.50 per week.	1
Therefore maximum allowable PHI benefit that could be paid would be up to 67% of £17,000 minus £3,510.	2
The maximum payment would therefore be up to £9,038 per annum.	1
May be even less than this if required to average income over last three years.	1
Mr Bennett is therefore paying for more permanent health insurance than he could actually claim.	2
The benefit should therefore be reduced.	1

10 marks

(ii) Options available to Mr Bennett to provide for life assurance cover

Level term assurance	1
Convertible term assurance	1
Pension term assurance	2
Any term acceptable up to 12 years	1
Unit linked whole of life assurance	1
Using standard or maximum sum assured basis	1
Reviewable term assurance	1
Family income benefit	1
Family income benefit written as pension term cover	1

10 marks

(iii) Most suitable

Any form of term assurance would be acceptable.	1
The most suitable would relate the suitable term to dependency of children.	2
The most suitable will be written as a pension term assurance, for cover for children.	2
Tax relief on premiums is available at marginal rate.	2

Mock exam 2 solutions Notes

(b) (i) **Further information/clarification required**

Required income in retirement	1
Expressed in today's terms	1
When would Mr Bennett actually wish to retire?	1
What is the value of the existing pension plan?	2
To what retirement age is the existing pension plan written?	1
What are the estimated benefits from the existing pension plan?	1
Was the existing Pension Plan changed to reflect Mr Bennett change of employment status from employed to self-employed?	2
So is monthly contribution of £80 net or gross?	1
How much would Mr Bennett be willing to increase his regular pension contributions by?	1
How much 'spare' income do Mr and Mrs Bennett have on a month to month basis?	1
Do Mr and Mrs Bennett have any other investments?	1
What is the Bennett's attitude to investment risk?	<u>1</u>
	14 marks

(ii)

Mr Bennett is age 48 so maximum permitted percentage of net relevant earnings to personal pension provision is 25% in respect of each of the current and last tax years	2
For 2000/01 25% of £17,000 equals £4,250	1
In respect of 1999/00 25% of £15,000 is £3,750	1
Total maximum is therefore £8,000.	1
Could all be paid in 2000/01 and allowable for tax in 2000/01 and 1999/00	1
Mr Bennett is a basic rate tax payer in respect of both tax years so the amount of tax relief is the same whichever approach is adopted	1
By making a previous year's election, tax relief may be available earlier in respect of the £3,750 applicable to 1999/00	1
There may be scope for carry forward of unused relief from the previous 6 (or 7) years.	1
This is subject to the full premium being paid for 2000/01	<u>1</u>
	10 marks

(c) **Portfolio of products**

Available to invest: £55,000	1
£8,000 should be invested into a single premium personal pension.	2
With the remaining £47,000 acceptable products would be Individual Savings Account - up to £7,000 each into a maxi – ISA.	2

Mock exam 2 solutions

Do not take account of emergency fund in amount available for investment.	1
National Savings Certificates 15th/51st Issue - up to £20,000	2
National Savings Capital Bonds - up to £10,000	2
Unit trusts subject to suitable risk profile - up to £10,000	2
No life assurance based products, eg investment bonds.	2
	14 marks

(d) **Factors to into take account**

Marketability of property	1
Cost of mortgage compared to cost of rent	2
Future maintenance costs	2
Type of mortgage	2
Acceptability of income to potential lender as borrower is self employed	1
Cost of life assurance to protect mortgage	1
Term over which any mortgage would be repaid	1
	10 marks

3 (a) **Factors that will influence the decision**

Requirement to increase net income by £300 per month	1
No risk to capital / clients of state of health	1
Age of clients	1
Future income to keep pace with inflation	1
Tax position of Mr and Mrs Green	1
Amount of emergency money/money for immediate access required.	1
	6 marks

(b) (i)

	Non savings income £	Savings income (gross) £	
State pension	5,611.00	5,000	1
Occupational pension	1,800.00		2
	7,411.00		
Aged persons allowance	(5,790.00)	5,000	
	1,621.00		
Tax on non savings			
£1,520 @ 10%	152.00		2
£101 @ 22%	22.00		2
Tax on savings income			
@ 20%	1000.00		
Less aged married couples			
allowance £5,185 @ 10%	(518.50)		2
	£655.50		
Income (£7,411 + £5,000)	12,411.00		
Tax	(655.50)		
After tax income	11,755.00		

Mock exam 2 solutions

(b) (ii) **Relevant tax related matters**

Mrs Green is making no use of her personal allowance	2
Mr Green is a basic rate tax payer	1
Mr Green is below age allowance trap threshold (£17,000 for 2000/01)	1
Any products generating taxable income should be in Mrs Green's name ...	1
... at least to the extent of using her personal tax allowance (£4,385 for 2000/01)	1

(iii) There is no unique, correct answer - the following can be used as a guide.

	OK for income	Max £	Min £	
Total for investment		125,000		1
Instant access Bank or Building Society	Y	10,000	1,800	1
Higher interest deposit account	Y	10,000	2,500	1
NSC 51st/15th Issue	N	10,000	2,000	2
Any ISA - (one each)	Y	7,000	3,000	2
NSC Income Bonds	Depends	7,000	1,200	1
With Profits/Managed Investment bonds	Y	50,000	2,500	2
g'teed income bonds	Y	15,000	3,500	2
Unit/investment trusts 3 or more funds	Y	15,000	3,500	1
Maximum of £5,000 in any single fund				1
Income must be in range £580 to £620 per Month from acceptable products as marked with Income from other products deducted for this purpose				2
Correct tax treatment for all products selected by candidate				2
Use of Mrs Green's tax allowance, putting income earnings products in her name				2

Maximum 16 marks

(c) **Reasons for product recommendation** to a maximum of 12 marks.

Instant access bank or building society
- Safe - no risk
- Emergency fund
- Feeder for future TESSA payments
- Feeder for future ISA payments
- Accessible

Higher interest deposit account
- Safe - no risk
- Emergency fund
- Feeder for future TESSA payments
- Feeder for future PEP payments
- Gives higher income than instant access account
- Accessible

NSC 51st/15th Issue
- Safe - no risk
- Guaranteed growth to provide secure (51st)/ Indexed (15th) growth
- Accessible after 5 years or earlier with penalties
- Fund available to reinvest at maturity to give more income

Maxi – ISA
- Tax free growth and income (*Not tax efficient* because withdrawing funds from a tax free roll-up product)
- Accessible
- Capital growth potential
- Income growth potential
- Spread of investment risk as unit trust based/cash and life assurance possible also.

NS Certificate Income Bonds
- Safe - no risk
- Competitive after tax income
- Accessible subject to notice

With profits/managed investment bonds
- Capital growth potential
- Accessible with possible penalties
- No further tax on gains for basic rate taxpayers
- Spread of investment risk

Guaranteed income bonds
- Safe
- Return of capital after selected term
- Regular and basic rate tax paid income
- Competitive after tax income

Unit/investment trusts
- Capital growth potential
- Income growth potential
- Opportunity to use CGT allowances
- Tax free growth in fund
- Spread of investment risk

Maximum of 3 marks for each product - overall maximum of 12 marks

SOLUTIONS TO

FINANCIAL PLANNING CERTIFICATE

PAPER 3

MOCK EXAM 3

Notes   **Mock exam 3 solutions**

FPC3 Exam 3 – Marking Scheme

(a) (i) **A total of 10 marks from the following**

Mr and Mrs Davison are married with 2 children	1
John Davison is aged 43, Brenda is 45	1
The 2 children are twins aged 21	
All of the family are said to be in good health	1
John Davison manages a large DIY Superstore	1
He is a member of the firm's pension scheme	1
John is covered by the firm's life assurance plan	1
The family is covered by the firm's private medical insurance plan	1
John has been employed by the same employer for the last 22 years	1
Brenda earns money through writing short stories	1
Brenda earns an average of £450 per month	1

Maximum 10 marks

(ii) **Financial objectives**

They are selling their main residence for £120,000	1
They have an outstanding mortgage of £40,000	1
Their mortgage repayments amount to £275 per month	1
John has an overdraft limit of £5,000	1
They have no HP or credit and pay their credit card balance each month	1
There is an endowment policy covering the existing mortgage. The policy is with Reliable Life, contributions are £60 per month.	1
A surrender value has been requested on the Reliable Life policy.	1
Brenda has a PEP savings plan. She saved £30 per month and believes the current value to be £3,000.	1
John has an endowment savings plan. He pays £10 per month, it is believed to be worth £22,000 when it matures at age 50.	1
John has a PHI policy for the maximum allowable amount.	1
John and Brenda have made wills.	1
They have at least £25,000 in a joint current account.	1

Maximum 8 marks

Mock exam 3 solutions   Notes

(iii) **Pension details**

John belongs to his employer's occupational pension scheme	1
The scheme accrual rate is 60ths	1
John expects to receive the maximum pension at age 65	1
	Maximum 3 marks

(iv) **Financial objectives**

John and Brenda wish to finance the purchase of their new home.	1
John and Brenda also wish to finance the cost of the modernisation work.	1
John and Brenda want to travel to Australia in 3 years' time.	1
John wishes to look at the possibility of early retirement.	1
	Maximum 3 marks

(v) **A total of 3 marks for a complete answer**

Current salary		£30,000.00	1
	× 66%	£20,000.00	
Less state benefits		£ 3,180.00	1
		£16,820.00	
	Divide by 52	£ 323.46 per week	1
		Maximum 3 marks	

(b) **Errors/inconsistencies (to a maximum of 10 marks)**

Tax relief is no longer available on mortgages. — 2

Brenda's PEP savings plan has only received 24 payments of £30 so the estimated value of £3,000 needs to be checked. Also, the reference to emerging markets may mean that it is not a PEP - PEPs must invest at least 50% in UK/EC equities in order for the fund to be qualifying. She will have to open an ISA if she wishes to continue saving. — 2

John Davison cannot be paying tax at 40% on all of his income as stated by Brenda. He is paying some tax at 40% on taxable earnings (after personal allowances) above £28,400. — 2

The pension scheme will provide the maximum pension at age 65. If John wishes to retire at 58, the maximum pension would reduce to 37/60ths and the scheme pension may well be less than that as a result of penalties — 2

If he takes the maximum 40/60ths pension, he is not able to also take the maximum tax-free cash sum. — 2

John believes that his firm covers him for life cover equal to twice his salary. His wife believes the factor to be six times. The Inland Revenue maximum is four times salary for death insurance lump sum benefit. — 2

Maximum 10 marks

(c) **Questions to ask Mr and Mrs Davison (maximum of 13 marks)**

We need to establish exactly how much comes into the household each month and how much of that you spend.	1
We need to identify how much surplus income you have.	1
What is John's net take home pay each month?	1
When was John's salary last reviewed - what happened?	1
Does John have any investment income?	1
Is Brenda self-employed?	1
Is there a pattern to the amounts that Brenda receives?	1
Does Brenda have any investment income?	1
Do you have any joint investment income?	1
Do you contribute anything towards your children's upkeep?	1
Exactly how much do you pay on your existing mortgage?	1
What type of mortgage do you have?	1
How much do you pay in premiums on the policy that supports the mortgage?	1
How much of your overdraft limit are you currently using?	1
How much do you pay on your overdraft each month?	1
How much do you pay on your credit card each month?	1
How much do you spend each month on heating, lighting, telephone and council tax?	1
How much do you spend each month on food, drink, clothing, entertaining etc?	1
How much do you save towards holidays each month?	1
How much are your motoring expenses each month?	1
Do you have any other regular outgoings?	1
How much does each of you allocate as spending money each month?	1

Maximum 13 marks

2

(a) **Factors to consider (to a maximum of 19 marks)**

What level of income would they require in order to maintain their desired standard of living?	2
When would they like to retire?	1
What state benefits will they qualify for when they retire?	1

Mock exam 3 solutions

Will they need to use savings and investments to supplement their retirement income to achieve their target?	2
Belinda could begin to fund a personal pension in her own right	2
Should Dennis remain contracted-out of SERPS?	1
How can they best utilise the available tax reliefs when investing in pensions?	2
Mr Allen will not receive state benefits until age 65, even if he retires earlier	1
What is their attitude to risk in the context of investing in a pension plan?	1
Mr and Mrs Allen should contribute as much as possible as early as possible in order to optimise the benefits they can expect at retirement	2
Are either Dennis or Belinda eligible to join an occupational pension scheme?	1
Do they require life cover to run alongside the pension?	1
Should Belinda contract out of SERPS?	1
Does Belinda have any existing pension arrangements?	1
	19 marks

(b) (i) **Contributions**

The maximum total contribution in the current tax year is limited to £19,000 gross, his net relevant earnings (using carry forward).	2
He contributes £960 net = £1,231 gross (960 × $\frac{100}{78}$)	2
Maximum this year = £19,000 less £1,231 = £17,769 gross	2
Less 22% tax relief = £13,859 net contribution for the current year	2
	8 marks

(ii) **Portfolio (to a maximum of 14 marks)**

There are a number of acceptable answers. Full marks will be awarded for a portfolio containing the following elements. Different products and different amounts may be used but the investment should be spread between Mr & Mrs Allen as shown.

		£	
Identify available investment	Inheritance	35,000	
	Emergency fund	750	
	Savings	3,500	
	Total	39,250	
			2
Investment split between Mr & Mrs Allen			2

Mock exam 3 solutions

		£	
For Mr Allen			
Single contribution to Personal Pension			
Managed Fund		13,859 (net)	2
XYZ UK Growth Maxi – ISA		7,000	2
National Savings Certificates 15th Issue		7,500	2
For Mrs Allen			
Baker Recovery Maxi – ISA		7,000	2
In joint names			1
Wessex Building Society Gold Account		3,891	
Total portfolio		39,250	1

14 marks

(c) **Justification for recommendation**

(i) Mr and Mrs Allen have a need for longer term investments, so the investment in the Pension and ISAs satisfies this requirement. — 3

NSCs, ISAs and pensions satisfy their expressed need for tax efficient investments. — 3

The investment portfolio and therefore the risk should be spread between a number of contracts, including the pension. — 3

NSC provide an element of security. — 2

Mr & Mrs Allen expressed a wish to increase the amount in emergency Fund — 2

15th issue NSC provide an index-linked return over 5 years. — 2

15 marks

(ii) **Justification for amounts**

The amount of single pension contribution is the maximum allowable. — 2

The amounts to be invested in equity based investments (ISA & Pension) represent approximately 70% of the total portfolio. — 2

The NSC investment inflation proofs part of the portfolio and allows accessibility to these funds. — 1

The ISA investment for Mr & Mrs Allen is the maximum allowable. — 1

6 marks

(iii) **Unused relief**

Any unused reliefs can be carried forward to the next tax year, when the client can review his needs. — 2

(d) (i) **Savings**

Mr Allen's pension contribution represents 5.05% of salary. The benefits at retirement unlikely to be sufficient for their needs. — 2

He is allowed to contribute 20% of salary. — 1

Mr Allen should increase his contribution by say £75 net per month. — 1

Mrs Allen is eligible to take out personal pension. — 1

Mrs Allen should contribute say £75 net per month to a personal pension   1

Mr and Mrs Allen should each invest £75 per month into ISA contracts (if they haven't already taken one out for the current tax year).   1

The balance of £50 per month should be saved in the building society either for future investments or to meet additional expenses.   <u>1</u>

8 marks

(ii) **Reviewing savings**

Undertake a regular review of their circumstances - at least once per year.   1

Confirm that Belinda is still in full time work and able to continue to save at the agreed level.   1

Ensure that the product portfolio continues to meet their needs.   <u>1</u>

3 marks

3 (a) Investment portfolio

(i) John wishes to invest for capital growth and has no requirement for an income.   1

He requires access to some of his capital in 5+ years time to fund the cost of buying into the partnership.   1

He has a balanced attitude to risk.   1

He is a higher rate taxpayer.   1

His circumstances may change in the future - eg possibility of marriage.   1

He wishes to retain some money in his current account and 'feed' the existing TESSA.   1

(ii) The most important factor is that he requires good capital growth and access to some capital in 5+ years time.   <u>2</u>

6 marks

(b) **Investment portfolio (to a maximum of 11 marks)**

There are a number of acceptable answers. Full marks will be awarded for a portfolio containing the following elements. Different products may be used but the amounts should be as those shown in the table.

	£	
Retain in current account	4,000	1
Wessex Building Society 90 day notice Account	8,800	1
Feeder Account for TESSA	4,200	1
Highwater Utilities Growth Maxi – ISA	7,000	1
National Savings Certificates 15th Issue	10,000	1
National Savings Certificates 51st Issue	10,000	1
Souwest Investment Trust	15,000	1
XYZ UK Growth Unit Trust	15,000	1
Reliable Unit Trust	15,000	1
Provident Recovery Unit Trust	<u>15,000</u>	1
Total available	£104,000	<u>1</u>

11 marks

(c) **Reasons for recommendations (up to 15 marks for (I) and 5 for (ii))**

Money in current account and in building society

(i)
- Security of capital — 1
- Money in building society is accessible within 90 days for emergency fund — 1
- The money could be used to fund the ISA in the future — 1

(ii) The amount recommended is approximately equal to 3-4 months salary — 1

Feeder account for TESSA

(i) Interest credited to the TESSA will be tax-free at the end of 5 years — 1

The capital in TESSA is secure and is available at the end of 5 years, (or option to re-invest in a Tessa-only ISA) — 1

Capital can be withdrawn before 5 years although tax benefits are lost from TESSA — 1

(ii) The amount recommended is the amount needed to fund the TESSA over the next three years to the maximum amount — 1

Maxi – ISA

(i) This product offers tax free income which may be reinvested. — 1
There is potential for long term capital growth. — 1
Withdrawals of capital may be made in the future without any tax liability. — 1

(ii) The amount recommended is the maximum allowed in a tax year. — 1

National Savings Certificates - both issues

(i) Both issues produce tax free growth over a five year period. — 1
The 15th issue offers growth at 1.65% p.a. above the rate of inflation. — 1
The capital is secure, (guaranteed by the Government). — 1

(ii) The amount recommended is the maximum amount allowed (other than re-investment). — 1

Investment trusts and unit trusts

(i) Four separate holdings offer a spread of investment risk through diversification — 1

The holdings may be transferred into a ISA in the future, if appropriate — 1

All of the funds offer potential for capital growth and relatively low yields, thereby keeping John's tax liability as low as possible — 1

(ii) The total amount invested means that approximately 60% of the total portfolio is invested for long term capital growth — 1

Maximum of 20 marks

(d) **Long term planning**

Undertake a regular review of his life assurance needs, especially if he is to be married — 1

Ensure that he is fully protected in the event of ill health — 1

Discuss the question of making a will. (If he gets married any will made whilst he was single will become void.)	1
Ensure that he is taking full advantage of tax-free investments each year ie he should invest the maximum allowed into TESSAs and ISAs	1
Ensure that he is aware of new issues of National Savings Certificates.	1
Review the pension scheme, looking, for example at FSAVC/AVC to cover benefits-in-kind and any non-pensionable earnings.	1
Try to utilise the CGT annual exemption by bed and breakfasting trusts and unit trusts so as to minimise John's liability to CGT (30 day gap between deals).	1
Ensure that sufficient funds are available when John is able to invest in the partnership.	1
Regularly monitor and review the performance of the portfolio.	1
Regularly review John's personal and financial situation to ensure that his requirements have not changed.	1
Regularly review the content of the portfolio to ensure that it continues to meet John's needs.	<u>1</u>
	11 marks

FPC3: Identifying and satisfying client needs (3/00)

ORDER FORM

BPP publish Study Texts and Kits for papers of the Financial Planning Certificate, the Advanced Financial Planning Certificate and SOFA Associateship/Fellowship. Each is, like this one, tailored precisely to the syllabus and contains plenty of practice material.

To order Study Texts or Kits, telephone us on 020-8740 2211. Alternatively, complete the order details below and send your order to us at the address shown or by fax on 020-8740 1184.

To: BPP Publishing Ltd, Aldine House, Aldine Place, London W12 8AW

Full name (Mr/Ms): _____

Daytime delivery address: _____

_____ Postcode: _____

Please send me the following books:

		Quantity	Total (£)
Financial Planning Certificate (5/99) Texts			
FP1: Financial Services and their Regulation	£25.95		
FP2: Protection, Savings and Investment Products	£25.95		
FP3: Identifying and Satisfying Client Needs	£25.95		
Financial Planning Certificate (1/00) Kits			
FP1: Practice and Revision Kit	£15.95		
FP2: Practice and Revision Kit	£15.95		
FP3: Practice and Revision Kit	£15.95		
Advanced Financial Planning Certificate (7/99) Texts			
G10: Taxation and Trusts	£32.95		
G20: Personal Investment Planning	£32.95		
G30: Business Financial Planning	£32.95		
G60: Pensions	£32.95		
G70: Investment Portfolio Management	£35.95		
G80: Long-term Care, Life and Health Protection	£35.95		
H25: Holistic Financial Planning	£35.95		
SOFA Associateship/Fellowship (7/99) Texts			
H15: Supervision and Sales Management	£35.95		
Advanced Financial Planning Certificate (1/00) Kits			
G10: Practice and Revision Kit	£19.95		
G60: Practice and Revision Kit	£19.95		
		Subtotal	

Postage and packaging
UK: £3 for first book, £2 for each extra   p & p
Europe (inc ROI & CI): £5 for first book, £4 for each extra
Rest of world: £20 for first books, £10 for each extra

Total

I enclose a cheque for £_____(Cheques to BPP Publishing Ltd) or charge to my **Access/Visa/Switch**

Card number □□□□ □□□□ □□□□ □□□□

Start date (Switch only) _____ **Expiry date** _____ **Issue no. (Switch only)** _____

Signature _____ **Daytime Tel. (for queries only)** _____

For Updates to your Study Text, visit our website: www.bpp-pub.demon.co.uk

FPC3: Identifying and satisfying client needs (3/00)

REVIEW FORM & FREE PRIZE DRAW

All original review forms from the entire BPP range, completed with genuine comments, will be entered into one of two draws on 31 July 2000 and 31 January 2001. The names on the first four forms picked out on each occasion will be sent a cheque for £50.

Name: _____   Address: _____

Date: _____

How have you used this Kit?
(Tick one box only)

☐ home study (book only)
☐ on a course: at _____
☐ with 'correspondence' package
☐ other _____

Why did you decide to purchase this Kit?
(Tick one box only)

☐ recommended by training department
☐ recommendation by friend/colleague
☐ recommendation by a lecturer at college
☐ saw advertising
☐ have used BPP Texts/Kits in the past
☐ Other _____

During the past six months do you recall *(Tick as many boxes as are relevant)*

☐ seeing our advertisement in *Financial Adviser*
☐ seeing our advertisement in *Money Management*
☐ seeing our advertisement in *IFA Contact*

Which (if any) aspects of our advertising do you find useful?
(Tick as many boxes as are relevant)

☐ prices and publication dates of new editions
☐ checklist of contents
☐ facility to order books off-the-page
☐ none of the above

Your ratings, comments and suggestions would be appreciated on the following areas.

	Very useful	Useful	Not useful
Introductory section	☐	☐	☐
Technical knowledge	☐	☐	☐
Practice examination	☐	☐	☐
Structure and presentation	☐	☐	☐
	☐	☐	☐

	Excellent	Good	Adequate	Poor
Overall opinion of this Kit	☐	☐	☐	☐

Do you intend to continue using BPP Study Kits/Texts?   ☐ Yes   ☐ No

Please note any further comments, suggestions and apparent errors on the reverse of this page, or write by e-mail to rogerpeskett@bpp.co.uk

Please return this form to: Roger Peskett, BPP Publishing Ltd, FREEPOST, London, W12 8BR

FPC3: Identifying and satisfying client needs (3/00)

REVIEW FORM & FREE PRIZE DRAW (continued)

Please note any further comments, suggestions and apparent errors below.

FREE PRIZE DRAW RULES

1. Closing date for 31 July 2000 draw is 30 June 2000. Closing date for 31 January 2001 draw is 31 December 2000.

2. Restricted to entries with UK and Eire addresses only. BPP employees, their families and business associates are excluded.

3. No purchase necessary. Entry forms are available upon request from BPP Publishing. No more than one entry per title, per person. Draw restricted to persons aged 16 and over.

4. Winners will be notified by post and receive their cheques not later than 6 weeks after the relevant draw date. Lists of winners will be published in BPP's *focus* newsletter following the relevant draw.

5. The decision of the promoter in all matters is final and binding. No correspondence will be entered into.